THE BEST
STAGE SCENES
FOR MEN
FROM THE 1980'S

JOCELYN A. BEARD has edited The Best Men's Stage Monologues of 1990 and The Best Women's Stage Monologues of 1990 (Smith and Kraus, Inc., 1991). She has also co-edited Contemporary Movie Monologues: A Sourcebook for Actors (Fawcett/Columbine, Spring 1991).

KRISTIN GRAHAM is a faculty member at Southern Connecticut State University where she teaches theatre history and acting. She belongs to the Theatre Artists Workshop of Westport, Connecticut. She co-edited Monologues from Literature: A Sourcebook for Actors (Fawcett/Columbine, 1990).

DES McANUFF has been the artistic director of the La Jolla Playhouse since its 1983 revival. He is an adjunct professor of theatre at UCSD and a former faculty member at The Juilliard School.

i

Other Books for Actors from Smith and Kraus

The Best Men's Stage Monologues of 1990
edited by Jocelyn Beard

The Best Women's Stage Monologues of 1990
edited by Jocelyn Beard

Street Talk: Character Monologues for Actors
by Glenn Alterman

Great Scenes for Young Actors from the Stage
Craig Slaight and Jack Sharrar, editors

The Best Stage Scenes for Women from the 1980's
edited by Jocelyn A. Beard and Kristin Graham

One Hundred Men's Stage Monologues from the 1980's
edited by Jocelyn A. Beard

One Hundred Women's Stage Monologues from the 1980's
edited by Jocelyn A. Beard

THE BEST
STAGE SCENES
FOR MEN
FROM THE 1980'S

Edited by
Jocelyn A. Beard
and
Kristin Graham

SK
A Smith and Kraus Book

A Smith and Kraus Book
Published by Smith and Kraus, Inc.

Copyright © 1991 by Smith and Kraus, Inc.
All rights reserved

Cover design by David Wise
Text design by Jeannette Champagne

Manufactured on recycled paper in the United States of America

First Edition: June 1991
10 9 8 7 6 5 4 3 2 1

Publisher's Cataloging in Publication
(Prepared by Quality Books Inc.)

The Best stage scenes for men from the 1980's / edited by Jocelyn A.
Beard and Kristin Graham. --
 p. cm.
 Includes bibliographical references.
 ISBN 0-9622722-8-0
 1. Acting. 2. Drama--Collections. I. Beard, Jocelyn A., 1955-
II. Graham, Kristin, 1951-

PN2080   808.82
                               91-60872

Smith and Kraus, Inc.
Main Street, P.O. Box 10, Newbury, Vermont 05051
(802) 866-5423

Quality Printing and binding by Eagle Printing Co., Inc., Albany, New York 12202, U.S.A

ACKNOWLEDGMENTS

Grateful thanks to the playwrights for making this book possible.
Jocelyn A. Beard would also like to thank Sean Bagley and Melette
Moffat for their help with this project.

CONTENTS

CONTENTS

CONTENTS

FOREWORD

The ever-changing nature of human relationships provides fascinating inspiration for playwrights as can be seen in the revelations—sometimes painful, sometimes joyous—occurring between two characters in a well-crafted scene.

Issues facing men in our society have changed significantly over the past decade or so and dramatists both here and abroad have labored to incorporate these issues into challenging character interconnections. The tragedy of AIDS as captured so eloquently by Robin Swados in *A Quiet End*; the intrigue of glastnost as explored by Lee Blessing in *A Walk in the Woods* and the shame of apartheit as it destroys friendships and lives in Athol Fugard's *My Children! My Africa!* all serve to help define our world and our part in it.

The scenes in this book, including scenes for two men as well as for one man and one woman, have been selected with every effort to provide actors with a wide range of characters, situations and moods; and it is my hope that by rehearsing and performing these scenes you will gain new and invaluable insight into the complexities of the human heart.

—Jocelyn A. Beard
Patterson, NY
April, 1991

INTRODUCTION

Finding solid, exciting, <u>new</u> audition material has always been a dreaded chore for actors. For students of theatre, there is also the constant search for fresh, challenging material to use in classes. This book, *The Best Stage Scenes for Men from the 1980's*, should serve both needs.

This anthology of scenes reflects a wide range of characters in many different styles so that an actor should be able to continue to use it as a resource for many years to come. Let me add that this book can also be a valuable resource for actresses, in that many of the scenes include women. For either sex, these scenes present a number of issues for actors, beginning or advanced: style, vulnerability, comedy, class, dialects—the challenges are endless. A number of my favorite plays of the decade are included, and I am particularly pleased that two of the selections, Lee Blessing's *A Walk in the Woods* and Athol Fugard's *My Children! My Africa!*, are drawn from plays that have been produced at the La Jolla Playhouse. The contrast between these two plays reflects the kind of diversity evident among the other selections, the diversity of a decentralized, pluralistic national theatre.

As a director, I often encounter the same pieces over and over in auditions, and needless to say, it is often due to actors culling pieces from monologue and scene books. This collection, however, is different in that, by virtue of its table of contents alone, it will lead you other places. Most of the playwrights included here have a significant body of work to choose from. Many plays included within these pages undoubtedly contain other scenes that could be of use to you. No scene book will ever do all of the work for you, nor should it. That is your work as an actor. It is my firm belief that in order to achieve a meaningful, truthful performance an actor must examine his own role and, in fact, all of the roles in a play in its entirety. The actor must continue to rigorously search for fresh, interesting material, but he can be helped along the way. I believe this collection is a path well worth exploring in your ongoing search.

—Des McAnuff
Artistic Director
La Jolla Playhouse

THE BEST
STAGE SCENES
FOR MEN
FROM THE 1980'S

SECTION I

One Man and One Woman

BETRAYAL
by Harold Pinter
A flat - Winter, 1975 - Emma (30's) - Jerry (40's)

Emma - A woman ending an affair
Jerry - Emma's lover

Emma and Jerry are coming to the end of their love affair.
They meet in the flat that they've kept for their clandestine
meetings and discuss what to do with it.

(Flat. 1975. Winter. Jerry and Emma. They are sitting. Silence.)
JERRY: What do you want to do then? *(Pause.)*
EMMA: I don't quite know what we're doing, any more, that's all.
JERRY: Mmnn. *(Pause.)*
EMMA: I mean, this flat...
JERRY: Yes.
EMMA: Can you actually remember when we were last here?
JERRY: In the summer, was it?
EMMA: Well, was it?
JERRY: I know it seems—
EMMA: It was the beginning of September.
JERRY: Well, that's summer, isn't it?
EMMA: It was actually extremely cold. It was early autumn.
JERRY: It's pretty cold now.
EMMA: We were going to get another electric fire.
JERRY: Yes, I never got that.
EMMA: Not much point in getting it if we're never here.
JERRY: We're here now.
EMMA: Not really. *(Silence.)*
JERRY: Well, things have changed. You've been so busy, your job,
and everything.
EMMA: Well, I know. But I mean, I like it. I want to do it.
JERRY: No, it's great. It's marvellous for you. But you're not—
EMMA: If you're running a gallery you've got to run it, you've got to
be there.
JERRY: But you're not free in the afternoons. Are you?

1

BETRAYAL

EMMA: No.

JERRY: So how can we meet?

EMMA: But look at the times you're out of the country. You're never here.

JERRY: But when I am here you're not free in the afternoons. So we can never meet.

EMMA: We can meet for lunch.

JERRY: We can meet for lunch but we can't come all the way out here for a quick lunch. I'm too old for that.

EMMA: I didn't suggest that. *(Pause.)* You see, in the past...we were inventive, we were determined, it was...it seemed impossible to meet...impossible...and yet we did. We met here, we took this flat and we met in this flat because we wanted to.

JERRY: It would not matter how much we wanted to if you're not free in the afternoons and I'm in America. *(Silence.)* Nights have always been out of the question and you know it. I have a family.

EMMA: I have a family too.

JERRY: I know that perfectly well. I might remind you that your husband is my oldest friend.

EMMA: What do you mean by that?

JERRY: I don't *mean* anything by it.

EMMA: But what are you trying to say by saying that?

JERRY: Jesus. I'm not *trying* to say anything. I've said precisely what I wanted to say.

EMMA: I see. *(Pause.)* The fact is that in the old days we used our imagination and we'd take a night and make an arrangement and go to an hotel.

JERRY: Yes. We did. *(Pause.)* But that was...in the main...before we got this flat.

EMMA: We haven't spent many nights...in this flat.

JERRY: No. *(Pause.)* Not many nights anywhere, really. *(Silence.)*

EMMA: Can you afford...to keep it going, month after month?

JERRY: Oh...

EMMA: It's a waste. Nobody comes here. I just can't bear to think about it, actually. Just...empty. All day and night. Day after day and night after night. I mean the crockery and the curtains and the bed-spread and everything. And the tablecloth I brought from Venice. *(Laughs.)* It's ridiculous. *(Pause.)* It's just...an empty home.

JERRY: It's not a home. *(Pause.)* I know... I know what you wanted...but it could never...actually be a home. You have a home. I have a home. With curtains, etcetera. And children. Two children in two homes. There are no children here, so it's not the same kind of home.

EMMA: It was never intended to be the same kind of home. Was it? *(Pause.)* You didn't ever see it as a home, in any sense, did you?

JERRY: No, I saw it as a flat...you know.

EMMA: For fucking.

JERRY: No, for loving.

EMMA: Well, there's not much of that left, is there? *(Silence.)*

JERRY: I don't think we don't love each other. *(Pause.)*

EMMA: Ah well. *(Pause.)* What will you do about all the...furniture?

JERRY: What?

EMMA: The contents. *(Silence.)*

JERRY: You know we can do something very simple, if we want to do it.

EMMA: You mean sell it to Mrs. Banks for a small sum and...and she can let it as a furnished flat?

JERRY: That's right. Wasn't the bed here?

EMMA: What?

JERRY: Wasn't it?

EMMA: We bought the bed. We bought everything. We bought the bed together.

JERRY: Ah. Yes. *(Emma stands.)*

EMMA: You'll make all the arrangements, then? With Mrs. Banks? *(Pause.)* I don't want anything. Nowhere I can put it, you see. I have a home, with tablecloths and all the rest of it.

JERRY: I'll go into it, with Mrs. Banks. There'll be a few quid, you know, so...

EMMA: No, I don't want any *cash*, thank you very much. *(Silence.*

BETRAYAL

She puts coat on.) I'm going now. *(He turns, looks at her.)* Oh here's my key. *(Takes out keyring, tries to take key from ring.)* Oh Christ. *(Struggles to take key from ring. Throws him the ring.)* You take it off. *(He catches it, looks at her.)* Can you just do it please? I'm picking up Charlotte from school. I'm taking her shopping. *(He takes key off.)* Do you realize this is an afternoon? It's the Gallery's afternoon off. That's why I'm here. We close every Thursday afternoon. Can I have my keyring? *(He gives it to her.)* Thanks. Listen. I think we've made absolutely the right decision. *(She goes. He stands.)*

BLACK MARKET
by Joe Sutton
Hell's Kitchen, NYC - Present - Joann (20's) - Bijan (30-40)

Joann - A young singer
Bijan - A mysterious Iranian

Joann and Hatch, her husband, have recently arrived in New York with the highest of expectations. Reality forces them to readjust their goals, however, and soon Hatch is selling items on the Black Market in hopes of networking his way into some cash. Eventually, they encounter the mysterious Bijan. Here, Bijan has appeared in their apartment while Hatch is out. Against her better judgement, Joann is intrigued by and attracted to this slippery man.

(She smiles. She exits. Bijan goes to the telephone. He pulls the phone as far as he can away from the bathroom. He dials.)
BIJAN: *(Curt)* Who is this? Where's Donnie? Well, when...what? Yes, tell him. Bijan. He'll know! *(Slight pause, extremely impatient)* Look now, Donnie, you can't do that. Because I'm relying on...I don't want it left to her. Or Lloyd. Now, I don't want to call again and have you out, do you understand!! Yes, let me speak to her. Rosie, dear. No, I'm not angry. I can't tell yet, it seems likely. Because it needs to be done and you're the one to do it. Because they know you. Now, please, don't...yes, all right. Oh, my dear, of course I do; you know that. *(Joann enters. She has fixed her hair. She watches Bijan. Bijan sees her. He is distracted by Joann's "beauty".)* I have to ring off now. Yes, I will. Yes. good-bye. *(Bijan smiles at Joann.)*
JOANN: Didn't boil?
BIJAN: Oh my, don't you look lovely.
JOANN: Did it?
BIJAN: Did what?
JOANN: Did it boil?
BIJAN: No. Not yet.
JOANN: You're making yourself right at home, I see.
BIJAN: I hope you don't mind.

5

BLACK MARKET

JOANN: No, I...want you to.

BIJAN: Bit of nasty business, I'm afraid.

JOANN: Are you hungry?

BIJAN: Not especially.

JOANN: Cause I was gonna make up some toast.

BIJAN: Please. Do. *(She slips past him. Bijan returns to the easy chair.)* You've done smashing work, I must say.

JOANN: I have?

BIJAN: To the apartment, yes.

JOANN: Oh.

BIJAN: Certainly I can't have been the first to tell you that.

JOANN: Well...

BIJAN: I didn't think so.

JOANN: When was the last time you was here?

BIJAN: Well, I haven't been.

JOANN: You haven't?

BIJAN: Not that I recall, no.

JOANN: Well then, how do you know?

BIJAN: How do I know what?

JOANN: How do you know the work I done?

BIJAN: Well, I assumed. Intuition, I suppose.

JOANN: Oh.

BIJAN: It really is quite beautiful. Feminine. That's what stands out. The mysterious touch of a woman.

JOANN: The wallpaper's new.

BIJAN: Is it?

JOANN: Um-hm. It was just paint before.

BIJAN: Oh, it's lovely. Truly. A most striking pattern.

JOANN: It's castles.

BIJAN: Oh yes. Like from the fairy tales?

JOANN: Yeah. Yeah, like that.

BIJAN: Do you believe in fairy tales?

JOANN: Uh-uh.

BIJAN: No?

JOANN: Do you?

BLACK MARKET

BIJAN: Sometimes, I do, yes.

(Joann has poured the water. Now, again, she snaps to and becomes alert.)

JOANN: What do you take?

BIJAN: Pardon?

JOANN: In your coffee.

BIJAN: I like it sweet.

JOANN: Two spoons?

BIJAN: Actually, if...

JOANN: Here. I'll let you do it yourself. *(Joann takes him the coffee and several packets of sugar. As he takes it from her, he again holds her hand.)*

BIJAN: You're really most kind. *(He releases her. After a moment, she retreats to her own cup.)*

JOANN: You say he didn't know?

BIJAN: Didn't..?

JOANN: Hatch. When he'd be back. My husband.

BIJAN: Oh. No. He didn't.

JOANN: He say where he was going?

BIJAN: Yes. Yes, that he did mention.

JOANN: Yeah?

BIJAN: But I'm not at liberty to say, I'm afraid.

JOANN: You can't tell me where...

BIJAN: No. I mean, yes. This is very tasty, I must say. *(Slight Pause.)*

JOANN: What, he just brought you here and—

BIJAN: No.

JOANN: You came to get him?

BIJAN: Not that either, really.

JOANN: Well then...

BIJAN: Tell me, do you enjoy my suit?

JOANN: What's that?

BIJAN: My suit. How do you find it?

JOANN: Looks nice.

BIJAN: Would you care to examine it more closely?

7

BLACK MARKET

JOANN: No, I...I can see it from here.

BIJAN: The cut, yes. But not the texture. *(He goes over to her.)* Touch it. *(Joann touches the lapel. She is very timid.)* When a man is wearing a suit like this, what should the woman he escorts be wearing?

JOANN: *(Whispered)* I don't know.

BIJAN: Well, imagine yourself. What would you wear?

JOANN: *(Hoarse)* It would be very beautiful.

BIJAN: Of course it would.

JOANN: And expensive. Real expensive.

BIJAN: Oh, I've no doubt.

JOANN: It would shimmer.

BIJAN: Would it?

JOANN: Uh-huh.

BIJAN: What color would it be?

JOANN: Yellow. That kind of...real...

BIJAN: Pale?

JOANN: Yeah.

BIJAN: Very pale?

JOANN: Um-hm.

BIJAN: Yes, I can see just what you mean.

JOANN: You can?

BIJAN: And I agree. I would choose exactly the same. *(Joann is now deeply entranced. Bijan is about to kiss her when she suddenly breaks away.)*

JOANN: Of course, we can't afford nothin' like that.

BIJAN: You haven't much money, I know. But you can afford a great deal more than that.

JOANN: How do you figure?

BIJAN: Your assets are considerable.

JOANN: They are?

BIJAN: Oh come. Am I telling you something you don't know?

JOANN: Is that what you sell? Dresses?

BIJAN: Why do you say that?

JOANN: Or you know someone who does.

BLACK MARKET

BIJAN: When I buy dresses, which I do infrequently, as you can imagine, it's from shops, not personal acquaintances. *(Slight pause.)*
JOANN: *(Quizzically)* What kind of name is that anyway? Bee-zhan.
BIJAN: Persian.
JOANN: What's that?
BIJAN: Iranian.
JOANN: *(Uncomprehending)* Oh.
BIJAN: Khomeini. Shah.
JOANN: Yeah, I know. You with them?
BIJAN: They are on different sides.
JOANN: Which one you with?
BIJAN: Shah is dead.
JOANN: So you're with the other?
BIJAN: No. *(Laughs slightly)* No.
JOANN: Is that funny?
BIJAN: It is a bit, yes.
JOANN: How come?
BIJAN: It's complicated. However, your toast has popped. *(Joann goes to the toaster.)*
JOANN: You want some?
BIJAN: No. Thank you. *(She butters, jellies, and then eats.)*
JOANN: So what are my assets?
BIJAN: Well, if I name them, and my list is not complete, you'll have me at a disadvantage. Won't you?
JOANN: You're real worried about that, I bet.
BIJAN: Oh yes. Don't think you can fool me with your tricks.
JOANN: *(Almost hurt.)* I'm not trying to fool you.
BIJAN: Oh, but you are.
JOANN: Look, I don't even know who you are. Or why you're here. How could—
BIJAN: But that's not true. You don't know precisely why I'm here. Or precisely who I am.
JOANN: But I got an idea.
BIJAN: I should think so.
JOANN: Rosie. *(Slight pause. Bijan chuckles.)*

9

BLACK MARKET

BIJAN: Tell me, Joann, have you traveled?

JOANN: Have I..?

BIJAN: Traveled. By aeroplane. Or railroad.

JOANN: We're not from here, if that's what you mean.

BIJAN: Have you been outside the U.S.?

JOANN: No.

BIJAN: But you do have your passport?

JOANN: Well—

BIJAN: No matter. It'll only take a few weeks.

JOANN: *(Vehement)* I don't want it!!

BIJAN: *(Smiles)* Why do you say that?

JOANN: Cause...cause I can't speak their language.

BIJAN: Well, perhaps they'll speak yours. I do.

JOANN: Is that what this is about?

BiJAN: In part.

JOANN: We're gonna have to?

BIJAN: You won't be forced to.

JOANN: To where?

BIJAN: Would that make a difference?

JOANN: I don't know. Maybe.

BIJAN: I am surprised.

JOANN: By what?

BIJAN: You're most resourceful, the two of you. Living by your wits.

JOANN: So?

BIJAN: That you'd be wary of travel is amusing.

JOANN: You're just used to it.

BIJAN: True. *(Bijan smiles. He lights another cigarette.)*

JOANN: Why can't you tell me where he is?

BIJAN: Because it's not important. And you don't really want to know.

JOANN: Are we waiting for him?

BIJAN: We can, if you like.

JOANN: Or else what?

BIJAN: Do you have something in mind?

JOANN: I'm asking you.

BLACK MARKET

BIJAN: It sounds as if you do.

JOANN: No, I...don't.

BIJAN: Pity. Then we wait. Shall I show you something in the meantime? *(Slight pause.)*

JOANN: *(Quiet)* Yeah, ok. *(Bijan reaches into his pocket. He takes out a jewelry box.)*

BIJAN: This I will not bring over to you. You must come here to see it. *(Bijan opens the box and, facing it towards himself and away from Joann, places it on the edge of the bed.)*

JOANN: I thought maybe you had something like that on you.

BIJAN: Something like what? You can't possibly see it from there.

JOANN: Just that box is enough.

BIJAN: Oh? Is there nothing inside of it?

JOANN: No, there's something inside, too.

BIJAN: But the box is what's important. Is that what you mean?

JOANN: There's only one thing comes in a box like that.

BIJAN: And what is that?

JOANN: Something real...pretty. Something...

BIJAN: Well, don't just stand there. Come over and see it. Or have you lost your nerve? *(Bijan reaches out, as if to take away the box.)*

JOANN: No!

BIJAN: Well then? *(Joann comes towards him. At first trying to keep her distance, she must eventually stand directly between Bijan and the bed. Once there, she stands for a long moment.)*

BIJAN: Please. Kneel down. *(Joann kneels.)* You may look as closely as you like. *(Joann reaches for the box tentatively. She inspects the contents, holding it for a very long time.)*

JOANN: Are they real?

BIJAN: Yes.

JOANN: You got others besides these?

BIJAN: Yes.

JOANN: Are they real, too?

BIJAN: Yes. *(Slight pause.)*

JOANN: Jesus. It's like there's magnets. I can't stop looking.

BIJAN: Joann, did you know there are bedspreads made of Mongolian

11

chinchilla costing upwards of a quarter million dollars?

JOANN: No.

BIJAN: Furthermore, because of the way the lining is attached, and because it's intended to match the room's decor, if the color of the room should change, the bedspread must be replaced.

JOANN: What does that mean?

BIJAN: There are many things people will buy. At a variety of prices.

JOANN: Uh-huh. *(She is still transfixed by the box. Bijan watches her.)*

BIJAN: Joann, look at me. *(It takes a moment, and she is afraid when she does, but finally Joann looks at him.)* Would you like to own these?

JOANN: What?

BIJAN: For your very own.

JOANN: I—

BIJAN: Can you even imagine such a thing?

JOANN: No.

BIJAN: It's like fairy tales, isn't it?

JOANN: Uh-huh.

BIJAN: Well, they're yours. *(Bijan reaches for her. She is absolutely stunned. He kisses her lightly, but for a long moment.)* Go on now. Put them away.

JOANN: Put them away?

BIJAN: Yes.

JOANN: You mean hide them?

BIJAN: We don't want anyone else to find them, do we?

JOANN: Not even Hatch?

BIJAN: Do you tell each other everything?

JOANN: Yeah.

BIJAN: Always?

JOANN: Yeah.

BIJAN: Is that about to change, do you think?

JOANN: I don't know.

BIJAN: You're really quite the coquette, aren't you?

JOANN: The what?

BLACK MARKET

BIJAN: Tell me, Joann, does he make you happy?

JOANN: Does...

BIJAN: Are you happy with him? Hatch.

JOANN: Yeah.

BIJAN: You are?

JOANN: Yeah, I...I'm all mixed up.

BIJAN: It's for you to decide, my dear. Would you like to share them with Hatch?

JOANN: I'm not sure.

BIJAN: Do you think he'd allow you to keep them?

JOANN: I—

BIJAN: Wouldn't he take them from you, and despite your protest, try to resell them?

JOANN: I guess.

BIJAN: Oh yes, he would. You may be sure of it. *(Slight pause. Joann stands.)*

JOANN: I got a place. With my stuff.

BIJAN: With your..?

JOANN: *(Holds up a tube of contraceptive gel.)* He doesn't go in here.

BIJAN: Splendid. *(Bijan gets up and goes to the door.)* When I return we'll talk more of—

JOANN: Where are you going?

BIJAN: Oh, I must leave you now.

JOANN: But I thought—

BIJAN: I'll be in touch.

JOANN: What about Hatch?

BIJAN: He doesn't know I was here.

JOANN: He doesn't?

BIJAN: No.

JOANN: But I thought—

BIJAN: Joann. Something very exciting is about to happen to you if you'll let it.

JOANN: Yeah?

BIJAN: Would you like that?

13

JOANN: Uh-huh.

BIJAN: I'll ring you later this evening. *(Bijan opens the door.)*

JOANN: Wait. I have to tell him.

BIJAN: *(Shrugs)* If you must.

JOANN: But what's that gonna mean?

BIJAN: To what?

JOANN: To what's gonna happen.

BIJAN: If you want him to be with you, he'll come along.

JOANN: But what about..?

BIJAN: Hm?

JOANN: Us.

BIJAN: That, too, will be arranged. As all things are possible. Ta.
(Bijan exits.)

CARELESS LOVE
by John Olive
Chicago - Present - Jack (30's) - Martha (20's)

Jack - A struggling actor
Martha - A young dancer

Her brief affair with Jack has left Martha pregnant. When she notifies her former lover of her condition, he responds coldly.

MARTHA: Hi!

JACK: *(slightly startled)* Oh, hi. I thought you weren't coming.

MARTHA: Birthday party started drinking champagne, and, well, you know...

JACK: Champagne drinkers.

MARTHA: Yeah.

JACK: Animals. *(short beat)* Well, I'm glad you came. Sit down.

MARTHA: Well, okay. *(SHE sits, and takes the script, opens it.)* This the new play?

JACK: Yeah.

MARTHA: "Little Criminals." *(pages through the script)* Which are you?

JACK: Andrew.

MARTHA: *(reads)* "Gone to seed attorney. Less intelligent than he thinks. Drinks." *(starts paging through the script)*

JACK: *(watches her for a short moment)* The first act is very weak. I'm not in it. *(pauses)* Page forty eight. *(MARTHA reads.)* I could recite it.

MARTHA: No.

JACK: Want a beer? *(reads from a card on the table)* Molson, Moosehead, Dab, Harp, Guiness, Bass, Dos Equis, Carta Blanca and please stop me, Marty, before I go entirely insane.

MARTHA: No, thanks, Jack, I don't want any beer.

JACK: Okay. *(reads again)* Inglenook, Blue Nun, Gallo. Marty.

MARTHA: Nothing.

JACK: Perrier? Virgin Mary? Coke?

MARTHA: Nothing.

CARELESS LOVE

(Beat. MARTHA continues to read. JACK gently takes the script from her hands, and sets it aside. MARTHA looks away; suddenly, SHE looks lonely, upset.)

JACK: Are you okay, Marty?

MARTHA: I'm fine.

JACK: Are you...sick at all? In the mornings or something?

MARTHA: Little bit. Mainly, I'm tired.

JACK: Do you feel like there's really something...I don't know, weird, going on with you body? Something basic?

MARTHA: I'm pregnant.

JACK: Oh, okay, right. *(takes a pull of his beer)* How 'bout those Cubbies? *(beat)* Marty. I'm sorry about the other day, if I behaved badly.

MARTHA: When?

JACK: The other day. At the theater. You remember the little scene at the theater?

MARTHA: Scene?

JACK: Well, whatever you want to call it, it was a scene. The folks at rehearsal were all moved.

MARTHA: You're a very good actor.

JACK: *(stares at her, shocked, then laughs)* Look, this is hard. I mean, normally this is something that happens between people who know each other pretty well.

MARTHA: I'm sorry this is hard for you.

JACK: Do you really hate me?

MARTHA: Not at all. You were a very good lover.

JACK: *(after a slight pause)* Okay. Do you need some money?

MARTHA: Money?

JACK: For...an abortion? All I wanna do is whatever's the right thing. *(quick beat)* You know Stuart, the guy I was talking to at rehearsal when you came in? After you...left, he said, "Well, Jack, are you going to do the right thing by that girl?" And I said, "Marry her?" He looks at me, big dramatic pause, and says, "Pay for her abortion." *(pause)* Well, anyway, do you need some money? I...got my checkbook.

16

CARELESS LOVE

MARTHA: *(not looking at JACK)* I made an appointment today, at Planned Parenthood.

JACK: Oh? They have abortions there? It's not just...pills and rubbers?

MARTHA: They have referrals to abortionists. They send you someplace else, to get the abortion. All they do is, they advise you.

JACK: *(after a slight pause)* When's the—?

MARTHA: *(overlapping JACK)* And if you need— *(stops)*

JACK: Go ahead.

MARTHA: And if you need money or something, they can advise you about that.

JACK: Well, I can pay for... I can help you pay for the—

MARTHA: It happens really fast. They stretch your vagina open, with a...thing. Then there's this long needle, they showed me one, they use it to inject Novacaine into your cervix. That part hurts. Then they stretch your cervix open, and then they...suck the baby out, with a vacuum. Then they scrape the rest of it out, then they suck it all clean, and that's it. Easy. *(pauses)* Then you have a lot of emotional problems afterwards, lots of...anxiety, because of all the... Well, I guess you lose a lot of hormones.

JACK: Do you want me to go down there with you?

(MARTHA laughs, abruptly and rather shrilly.)

JACK: What's so funny?

MARTHA: That's not what you're supposed to say!

JACK: Tell me what I'm supposed to say! Tell me what to do! This is hard! You feel like a total stranger to me, and you wouldn't believe the load of Irish Catholic guilt I'm carrying about this.

MARTHA: You get guilty, I get pregnant.

JACK: *(Now JACK bursts out laughing. Then an abrupt beat: HE covers his face with his hands, weeping. Finally:)* Well, fuck you. You have as much responsibility in this as I do.

MARTHA: I don't expect anything from you. If all you want is for this to be over, then okay, it's over. I won't bother you any more. The guilt is your problem, I'm sure you can take care of that alone, I'm sure you've had lots of practice.

17

CARELESS LOVE

JACK: *(staring at her)* Jesus Christ.

MARTHA: I only told you because I thought you had a right to know.

JACK: As the father.

MARTHA: Yes.

JACK: You know, Marty, I was given to understand that your sex life was pretty varied and active, as they say.

MARTHA: Who gave you to understand that?

JACK: Persons who would, at this point, I'm sure, prefer to remain anonymous.

MARTHA: Well, they were wrong! You're the first person I've made love with since I left school.

JACK: Since...?

MARTHA: Almost three years.

JACK: That's great! Luck 'o the Irish, eh? Your first time out in three years and you get zapped!

MARTHA: I'm not Irish.

JACK: But I am! *(stands abruptly)* Well, you're not getting shit from me, the price of an abortion, and that's it. *(brandishes his script)* I got work to do! Gotta go fake and bullshit my way through another piece of shit play, the ole crazed Celtic charm strikes again. I should thank you, I'll be able to use all this in Act Three! *(starts to exit, then turns; in a fake-theatrical voice)* Good-bye, darling!

EACH DAY DIES WITH SLEEP
by José Rivera
New York - Present - Nelly (20's) - Johnny (20's)

Nelly - A much abused daughter of a domestic tyrant
Johnny - Nelly's lover

Nelly is the loyal daughter of Augie, a brutal man who has sired uncountable children and slept with as many women. Nelly is the only of his progeny to devote her life to serving him, until the arrival of Johnny, a man who has dated all of her sisters and who now casts his eye upon her. Here, Johnny convinces Nelly that he loves her.

(Johnny gets down on his belly and crawls across the floor, commando style. The face of a very pretty young woman, with the word "Gloria" over it, is projected. Nelly sees Johnny and jumps on his back, squashing him. She laughs.)
NELLY: You got teflon balls, little horsie! Big metal balls!
JOHNNY: GET OFF MY BACK, NELLY!
NELLY: Where to? Upstairs? Five o'clock in the morning, Johnny??
JOHNNY: Felicia's room—
NELLY: *Felicia's!?* You dumped Lizbeth so soon?! *(Hitting him)* Slime! Disease! Pestilence! *(Nelly goes to Augie's door and pounds on it)* Hey Dad! Wake up! *(Johnny grabs Nelly and pulls her away from the door. They struggle violently.)*
JOHNNY: Hey! I don't want your son-of-a-bitch father to see me! *(Johnny pins her down. He's on top of her. They look at each other. Johnny tries to kiss her. She pushes his mouth away.)*
NELLY: YUCK! YOUR SPIT TASTES LIKE GASOLINE! *(She bites him on the arm. He yowls and jumps off her, rubbing his arm in pain.)*
JOHNNY: So? I love you. Those weird-color eyes of yours make me nuts. Admit you love me.
NELLY: Admit all your bastards. Felicia's three kids! Maritza's twins! Nilda's retarded son! Yours!
JOHNNY: Will you slow *down*? You think too fast for your mouth—.

19

EACH DAY DIES WITH SLEEP

NELLY: My nieces and nephews are all your babies—.

JOHNNY: Oh man. That's beat. That's just a rumor.

NELLY: Bastards play guitar. Flex muscles. Comb hair. Like you do.

JOHNNY: *(combing hair)* Coincidence. *(He smiles at her. She scampers away. He follows.)* Awwww, just admit you love me, Nelly, c'mon.

NELLY: Oh. Go to Felicia. I don't care.

JOHNNY: I can skip Felicia. I always thought you were prettier. Just thought you were too young and weird—.

NELLY: My birthday today! I got no presents!

JOHNNY: I'm your present. I know you look at me. A guy can tell. You're not the pinhead everyone says.

NELLY: AM NOT STUPID.

JOHNNY: And you get me riled the way you crawl around on all fours and misuse your pronouns. You think I'm good looking? Do you?

NELLY: *(soft)* Maybe. I don't know. Don't trust you. *(Johnny comes toward Nelly again, but she runs away, pointing at the projection.)* No! You love Gloria.

JOHNNY: Gloria? No! She's a, she's a *girl*. Sixteen. A stick.

NELLY: You're killing time—waiting for puberty to explode her— you'll pounce her bones and forget me—.

JOHNNY: I've been waiting for *you*! To walk and talk right. I see improvement. I know just being with me is making you better all the time. *(He tries to touch her)* Nelly, Nelly, I play guitar like the wind. *(Nelly Stands completely straight for the first time in the play. It's a struggle. He looks at her extremely surprised.)*

NELLY: You hurt Maritza, then Nilda, then Lizbeth, then Felicia. A DISGUSTING TRACK RECORD.

JOHNNY: But don't you think I'm beautiful? *(She's back on all fours. She plays with the truck, ignoring him, which he can't stand.)* You're right. I made it with all your big sisters. I knocked them all up. What can I say? I love this family. *(Nelly turns away disgusted)* I can't help what nature's done to me. It's some magic I got. I'm a victim. I'm too beautiful to live. *(Johnny grabs her, holding her still)* You make

20

me feel different than your sisters do. I never met a woman who could resist me. How come you're the only one? You know how crazy that makes me get? *(He tries to kiss her, she pulls away)*

NELLY: I WILL NOT BE YOUR NEXT CASUALTY!

JOHNNY: Boy, your syntax has really picked up—.

NELLY: If Nelly and Johnny...*exist*...the buck stops here. No Gloria after me. I am forever or nothing.

JOHNNY: That's a long time—.

NELLY: Not worth it? Think about this. *(Nelly kisses him visciously. Then she pushes him away roughly. The kiss stuns Johnny.)* That's so—you know what—you give up—if you hurt me. *(She kisses him again. She is tender. She pushes him away tenderly.)* That's. A memory of me. Burned in your skin. Nerves will haunt you with that memory, drive you to a crazy suicide—and blast you—to a million, lovesick stars. *(Nelly crawls to the socks. Johnny is reeling from her kiss.)*

JOHNNY: What'd you do to my mouth? *That wasn't human, Nelly—*!

NELLY: *(dismissing him)* Felicia? Waiting?

JOHNNY: How can I kiss Felicia after this? You ruined me!

NELLY: *(pointing at projection)* Gloria? Bitch?

JOHNNY: Gloria who? Nelly, let's get married, tonight, please, we gotta. *(Nelly laughs.)* Hey, this isn't easy for me, so DON'T LAUGH. The truth is, I'm getting too old for this. Breaking into your father's castle, slithering up endless flights of stairs, through gloomy bedrooms and weird animals. I need you to help me grow up, like I'm helping you talk. *(Johnny kisses Nelly. She continues working on the socks, unfazed.)* C'mon, what do you want from me?

NELLY: Employment history. I want to know your prospects.

JOHNNY: My what?

NELLY: Johnny. I'm the—middle—child of twenty-one—number eleven. *I haven't left this house in two years.* NO MORE! Have to know what I'm getting into with you. Want prospects. Want better.

JOHNNY: I have prospects. I'm going to quit working on cars and make money on my knock-out looks. Be a fashion model.

NELLY: No prospects. *(She angrily grabs him by the lapels and*

EACH DAY DIES WITH SLEEP

shakes him) I HAVE IDEAS! Ideas bursting my skull open to *make* something. Don't want to watch and worry over brothers and sisters the rest of a—short—life.

JOHNNY: Like what ideas?

NELLY: My plan is this: I can fall asleep and dream winning lottery numbers. Can win big bucks real fast.

JOHNNY: You can?

NELLY: Make big bucks. Move to California. Open a garage. Fix Porsches, Mercedes, Jaguars. You and me. A team and we'll be rich, Johnny.

JOHNNY: But fixing cars is so *boring...*

NELLY: *Want* boring. Too much excitement in my life. Don't want more violence, hunger, and screaming babies. Want to sleep eight hours a day. Every day of the week. Johnny. *(She touches his face tenderly)* You're thirty-one. Still living with your Mami. Don't have the drive. I have the drive. *I want to go.* Go together?

JOHNNY: Are you using me? *(Nelly enthusiastically nods yes)* But you don't need me. You can walk out of here without me.

NELLY: *Do!* Do you notice? My brothers and sisters never leave? Why? My father's tyrant-blood is in us. His blood controls us. Keeps us afraid.

JOHNNY: I'm not afraid of him.

NELLY: I know! Your hate of him is in my blood now. It's going to help me escape him. *(Nelly kisses Johnny. The projection of Gloria disappears. Nelly smiles.)* Want you. Marry you.

JOHNNY: No Nelly. "I want to marry you." Say.

NELLY: "I want to marry you."

JOHNNY: I want to marry you. I want to have sex with you first.

NELLY: I can't sex here. Have no bedroom here. Every night, I wander. From room to room. Looking for pieces of floor not covered by members of my big family or animal droppings. But even in this house, its hundred rooms, I share space with somebody. If I *do* fall asleep, can't rest. My different color eyes are always in conflict and they keep me awake. *(Nelly stands up and walks normally, though with some effort. Her speech is nearly flawless.)* The blue eye hates the

EACH DAY DIES WITH SLEEP

grey eye for something the grey eye did to the blue eye when I was still a fetus floating like a little fish in my mother's huge body. Floating there among the schools of unborn brothers and sisters. Today, the fighting between my eyes gives me headaches, Johnny, and prophetic dreams. *(She smiles at him)* Help me rest. I'll stop using you. I'll love you—fiercely—the rest of my life.

JOHNNY: I think you're beautiful. Do you think I'm beautiful?

NELLY: Right now? I think you're very, very... *(Nelly falls asleep. Johnny lifts her and starts to carry her offstage. As he approaches the exit, the projection of Gloria comes back on. Johnny stops to look at the beautiful Gloria.)*

EASTERN STANDARD
by Richard Greenberg
A house on Fire Island - Present - Stephen (30) - Phoebe (20's-30)

Stephen - An architect who despises his job
Phoebe - A Wall Street broker

Six people meet in a restaurant in New York City and become
friends. Stephen falls in love with Phoebe. Drew, Stephen's
gay friend, is attracted to Phoebe's brother, Peter. Ellen, a
waitress, and May, a schizophrenic street person, are drawn into
the group who gather at Stephen's summer home on Fire Island.
Here, Phoebe has left Stephen to attend to a former lover who
she thinks has tried to commit suicide. She has just returned to
Stephen, having cut all ties to her former lover.

PHOEBE: Oh...hi!
STEPHEN: *(Turns, as if surprised.)* Oh, hi.
PHOEBE: I didn't expect to see you out here.
STEPHEN: I was...standing here.
PHOEBE: Yes.
STEPHEN: You're back.
PHOEBE: Yes. *(Beat.)*
STEPHEN: Do you want some coffee?
PHOEBE: No, thanks. Is Peter here?
STEPHEN: He and Drew are— *(Gestures vaguely in their direction.)*
PHOEBE: Oh... *(Beat.)*
STEPHEN: Did you have a good trip?
PHOEBE: Umm—
STEPHEN: I mean, on the bus coming back?
PHOEBE: Uneventful.
STEPHEN: Good.
PHOEBE: Well...
STEPHEN: And the trip going?
PHOEBE: The same.
STEPHEN: And the time there, what about the time there, was that—?
PHOEBE: Stephen—

24

STEPHEN: Was that uneventful, too?

PHOEBE: Quite.

STEPHEN: ...Really?

PHOEBE: Yes. *(Beat.)*

STEPHEN: In what way?

PHOEBE: In what way was it uneventful, that's hard to say, actually.

STEPHEN: Oh God, Phoebe—

PHOEBE: There were no scars, you'll be glad to know—no nausea from the stomach pump, no rope burns—

STEPHEN: It sounds like there was no—

PHOEBE: —no sucide attempt, yes.

STEPHEN: ...What?

PHOEBE: It was a ploy to get me to see him—

STEPHEN: That's amazing. When did you realize?

PHOEBE: When he told me.

STEPHEN: He *told* you?

PHOEBE: He thought I would be charmed.

STEPHEN: He thought—were you?

PHOEBE: For a second.

STEPHEN: My God!

PHOEBE: And then I was relieved!

STEPHEN: Relieved?

PHOEBE: Because for the first time I looked at him and I knew that there wasn't anything worthwhile about him. I was so sure I didn't have enough will to leave him twice, but I did, I did! I walked right out of that room and went straight to this restaurant where everyone I know goes. And I sat there by myself and I ordered and I ate very nicely.

STEPHEN: Huh.

PHOEBE: Everyone was thinking, "Boy, she got away with murder"— but I didn't care. And, Stephen, it was triumphant—because everything I thought was inevitable didn't happen! *(Sees his worried expression.)* What's wrong?

STEPHEN: You didn't come back here until a few minutes ago.

PHOEBE: So?

STEPHEN: There's a whole evening you haven't accounted for, yet.

PHOEBE: Yes. Well. I just sat in my apartment. I sat all night and listened to the phone ring—

STEPHEN: I'll bet.

PHOEBE: I didn't even *flinch*. And it was as though some sort of evil enchantment had been broken. I don't know why Loomis expected me to be charmed by a compulsive liar *or* an attempted suicide. I've come to realize neither interests me. And right now I can't imagine getting involved with either.

STEPHEN: You can't?

PHOEBE: No. *(Beat.)*

STEPHEN: Well, you have. With both...

PHOEBE: What do you mean?

STEPHEN: Should I tell you this?

PHOEBE: You might as well. I'm shockproof at this point.

STEPHEN: Oh Christ...the night before we finally met...I tried to...do myself in. *(Beat.)*

PHOEBE: What?

STEPHEN: With pills.

PHOEBE: For real?

STEPHEN: It was a farce, but I guess it has to count for real, yes...

PHOEBE: God.

STEPHEN: Things had been so bleak so long—

PHOEBE: Jesus—

STEPHEN: I meant to tell you eventually. I didn't realize it was a particular aversion.

PHOEBE: Well, I didn't either until—

STEPHEN: Well, there you are... *(Beat.)*

PHOEBE: So this is what my life comes down to? Two men who flirt with self-extinction like it's going to the movies?

STEPHEN: I guess so. What are you going to do about it? *(She goes to him, starts to kiss him; he pulls away.)* I'm sorry, I can't accept your terms!

PHOEBE: What?

STEPHEN: It's impossible. I mean you lie to me all summer and you leave and you come back the next day and in between you say you've had this huge revelation. But how do I know it's going to stick? Any minute you could run out on me, and then where would I be?

PHOEBE: That's true.

STEPHEN: You could run back to Loomis—

PHOEBE: Easily. Or I could just get tired of you.

STEPHEN: Yes, sure—

PHOEBE: Or I could become sick and die—

STEPHEN: No, don't say that—

PHOEBE: That happens all the time, believe me. Or you could fall out of love with me. Or we could be murdered in the street. Or we could just discover we're not who we think we are and go numb—

STEPHEN: Any of this—

PHOEBE: Drastic things will happen to us, so why not marry me? *(Beat.)*

STEPHEN: What?

PHOEBE: I'd like to have you around for a while.

STEPHEN: *(Amazed at her gall.)* You're really...something, you know that? *(Beat.)* You were right about Ellen. She put the moves on me last night.

PHOEBE: I'm not surprised.

STEPHEN: She said wonderful things about me. Much more enthusiastic than you've ever been.

PHOEBE: I'm sure that she—

STEPHEN: She went on and on, it was fantastic, it was irresistible—

PHOEBE: I understand that you were—

STEPHEN: I turned her down.

PHOEBE: What?

STEPHEN: She's gone now. You were off to Loomis and I turned her down. That was one of the few times in my life I've ever been *vied* for and—

PHOEBE: You're a fool—

STEPHEN: I'm a fool. I'm the biggest fool I've ever... Did you just ask me to marry you?

PHOEBE: Uh-huh...

STEPHEN: Why *me*?

PHOEBE: Because you're there.

STEPHEN: What?

PHOEBE: I wish I could say it was fate, or something romantic like that, but I can't. I don't know if I came to you by some inevitable path or if you're just where I landed, but you're there and I'm ready and it's a dangerous time and I love you, so what do you say? *(By this time, she's in tears.)*

STEPHEN: *(Slowly, but inevitably, going to embrace her.)* I'm not sure. God, I don't know. I'd hoped for something better.

FORGIVING TYPHOID MARY
by Mark St. Germain
N. Brother Island, NY - 1909-10 - Mary (30-40) - Father (40-50)

Mary Mullen - A carrier of typhus
Father McKuen - A visiting priest

Mary has been confined by the State of New York to a cottage on North Brother Island. Here she is visited by Father Michael McKuen of the Bronx, who feels compassion for one cast out of society through no fault of her own. Her bitterness is evident as she reminds the good father who it was that made the germs which she carries.

MARY: I want to ask you some questions about God.

FATHER: I hope I have some answers.

MARY: So do I. But before we talk I want you to promise me something.

FATHER: Yes?

MARY: Whatever we say stays between us. Private. Like a confession.

FATHER: Confidential. Of course.

MARY: What would happen if you lied to me about that?

FATHER: I wouldn't lie.

MARY: What if you did; how mortal a sin is it?

FATHER: I'd be violating my vows.

MARY: Would you go to hell?

FATHER: I could.

MARY: Good enough.

FATHER: I don't know. God can forgive anything we do.

MARY: That's the rumor.

FATHER: It isn't a rumor, it's a fact. It's why Christ died for us.

MARY: There are so many facts in the world, you'd think people would know more, wouldn't you? *(Picks up crocheting)* Would you like a doily?

FATHER: No, thank you.

MARY: I've been thinking about death. *(Pause)* And about God.

FORGIVING TYPHOID MARY

Do you believe in germs?

FATHER: I suppose I do. Yes.

MARY: Have you ever seen one?

FATHER: No. But I believe what I read about them. I believe they exist.

MARY: Like God.

FATHER: I wouldn't equate the two—

MARY: But God made germs because he made everything.

FATHER: Of course.

MARY: And everything God made is good.

FATHER: Yes.

MARY: So germs are good.

FATHER: Well...

MARY: Germs are His creatures the same as the lion, the bear and the housecat.

FATHER: I suppose they are.

MARY: Then God must love them as he loves his other creatures. As he loves Man.

FATHER: No; I really don't think God loves sickness.

MARY: No? *(She picks up her BIBLE, turns to a passage)*
"So angry was the Lord that when
he departed and the cloud withdrew from the tent,
there was Mariam, a snow white leper. Then Moses
cried to the Lord, Please, not this, pray, heal
her—"

(MARY puts down book) He didn't. But he did that to her, God.

FATHER: *(Interrupting)* Yes, Mary, but Jesus also cured the sick.

MARY: *(Pause)* Not all of them.

FATHER: He cured the lepers, the blind, the crippled...

MARY: He didn't cure all of them! *(Looks quickly into the Bible, marks a passage, hands it to FATHER)* Look there. Read.

FATHER:
"Now when it was evening and the sun had set,
they brought to him all who were ill and possessed.
And he cured many who were affected—"

FORGIVING TYPHOID MARY

MARY: "Many", it says. He cured "Many". So there were those he did not cure. Or would not cure.

("SARAH's MUSIC begins to underscore following section: MARY is less conscious of the Priest's presence, she is explaining to herself)

FATHER: Mary, what are you saying?

MARY: I was a cook.

(SARAH appears. In her lap is a near empty bowl of cake frosting. She rubs her fingers around the side of the bowl, eating what frosting she can get)

MARY: A good cook, too; ask any of them. No complaints. Second helpings. They looked forward to their meals. Their deserts. I made that food. But I didn't make their germs. Only God could do that. They weren't all sick, you know. And not all of them died.

FATHER: I don't understand.

MARY: God calls us to him at different times. We don't know his plans, his reasons.

FATHER: Of course not.

MARY: We all die. What's a day or a lifetime when we know in the end we'll all be called to God?

GAL BABY
by Sandra Deer
Georgia - Present - Gal Baby (40's) - Tommy (40's)

Gal Baby - An insinkable Southern Belle
Tommy - Gal Baby's philandering husband

It's been an exhausting day for Gal Baby, a feisty Georgia Peach who has just discovered that her mortgaged plantation has been lost in a fire, her Uncle has written a sleazy best-seller using her as a model for the lusty heroine, and her husband, Tommy, is having an affair. The remarkable Gal Baby does her best to take this all in stride, however, and here she and Tommy discuss his affair and his reluctance to end it.

GAL BABY: You were magnificent this afternoon, Tommy. Telling everybody what to do, and getting the animals out of the barn and all. I was proud of you.

TOMMY: Thank you, Gal.

GAL BABY: It reminded me of that time when we lost Mercedes in the shopping mall. You remember that? I was pregnant with Tommy Jr., and I was just about hysterical. Thinking somebody had taken my little girl. But you just stayed calm, and talked to the security people, describing what she was wearing.

TOMMY: Red corduroy overalls and a white tee shirt.

GAL BABY: You kept looking over at me and saying, "Everything's going to be all right, Sweetheart. Don't worry. We're gonna find her." You were so brave.

TOMMY: Well, we did, didn't we?

GAL BABY: I promised God if he'd just let my little girl be safe, I'd never ask him for another thing. I haven't kept that promise.

TOMMY: Everything's going to be all right, sweetheart.

GAL BABY: Is it? I'm so tired, Tommy. It seems like I've been fixing things forever. And they don't stay fixed. They just don't.

TOMMY: Gal, I'm... I want to be the guy I was this afternoon. You could be in love with that guy. Right?

GAL BABY: Uh huh.

GAL BABY

TOMMY: I want to be like that. All the time.

GAL BABY: I can see where you would. Tommy, when we were younger... Would you say I was a "wild thing?"

TOMMY: Oh, yes you were. The sweetest, wildest thing I ever knew.

GAL BABY: What happened? When did it...

TOMMY: I don't know, honey. Maybe it's not too late. Maybe... Gal, I don't know what's going to happen.

GAL BABY: Well, Tommy, if you don't know, who should we ask?

TOMMY: I wish I could say it's over. I won't ever see her again. But I'm not sure I could stick to it. Not yet. I just...

GAL BABY: Have to play the hand out.

TOMMY: Yes... I think I'll go clean up. *(Tommy turns, goes inside. Gal looks after him for a second.)*

GAL BABY: *(to audience)* Sometimes things just change. For no reason. Not because you did something wrong. They just change. Because they do. Because life's like that. What are you supposed to do when that happens? *(She turns, looks toward the window where Tommy's shadow has just appeared.)* I loved you, Tommy. You were the boy of my dreams.

THE HAVE-LITTLE
by Migdalia Cruz
South Bronx - 1974-1976 - Lillian (13-15) - José (36-38)
Lillian Rivera - A Puerto Rican girl, innocent and spiritual
José Rivera - Lillian's father, a charming brute
Here, Lillian's drunken father, José comes to her apartment to
visit.

*(LILLIAN opens the front door. JOSÉ stands there, all cleaned up and
in a new suit.)*
JOSÉ: Baby!
LILLIAN: Papi?
JOSÉ: Well, yeah. Do I look so different?
LILLIAN: Yeah, you do. *(JOSÉ sits on the armchair.)*
JOSÉ: So where is he? *(LILLIAN gets JOEY from the bedroom and
hands him to JOSÉ.)*
LILLIAN: He saved my life.
JOSÉ: All by himself? What's his name?
LILLIAN: Joey.
JOSÉ: Joey?
LILLIAN: Joey Rivera. Hard to remember, ain't it?
JOSÉ: Joey...Joey. That's not bad. Sounds like José.
LILLIAN: That's what it is, Pa.
JOSÉ: Lily, look at those arms! This boy's gonna be a boxer, like his
grandpa. *(HE offers the baby his finger.)* Ah! Look how he holds my
hand! Another Hercules! *(Pause)*
LILLIAN: I need money, papi. You have some? You look like you
do.
JOSÉ: Yeah, I got some. I got a job now. I'm working in the
building.
LILLIAN: I never asked you before but I need it for Joey. I can't go
back to work yet and I—
JOSÉ: How much do you want?
LILLIAN: How much you got?
JOSÉ: I'm not going to give it you—I'll give it to him.
LILLIAN: He'll give it to me. Right, Joey? He loves his mommy.
JOSÉ: What does he need? I'll go buy it. I wouldn't give you any
cash. Who knows what you would buy? Drugs or—

34

THE HAVE-LITTLE

LILLIAN: I don't do that. Can't you even tell that much?

JOSÉ: We should toast to his health, Lily. Don't tell me you don't drink.

LILLIAN: Just a little. *(HE gets a bottle of rum and two glasses)* It makes the baby sleepy.

JOSÉ: What?

LILLIAN: It goes into his milk and then he gets drunk or somefin. They explained to me at the hospital. I'm not supposed to get drunk no more.

JOSÉ: Incredible! *(Raising his glass and rising to his feet)* To Joey Hercules Rivera. May his life be better than ours. Better than his mami's and better than his grandma's. Better than his grandpa's and his grandpa's mami.

LILLIAN: Amen. *(SHE reaches for the baby)*

JOSÉ: What! You think I can't hold my own grandson? I'm drunk but I'm not stupid.

LILLIAN: Sit down, Pa.

JOSÉ: Alright. I'll sit down... *(HE sits and cradles the baby in his arms quietly)* So how is your mother? They say she's very sick.

LILLIAN: Papi...let me take him. It's almost time for his milk.

JOSÉ: He's alright. See? He likes me. I put him to sleep.

LILLIAN: Your breaf probably knocked him out.

JOSÉ: It's good for him to sleep. I like to sleep. Tell me about your mother.

LILLIAN: She's dead, pa. She's been dead for three months already. Don't you remember? We did the rosario by her grave? Don't you remember? I came to get you and you wore the blue suit papabuelo left you and we went to the cemetary. *(A slience)*

JOSÉ: *(HE strokes his forehead and hair)* She was a good woman, your mother.

LILLIAN: Then why din't you go see her?

JOSÉ: What could I've done for her?

LILLIAN: Nuffin. Just go see her.

JOSÉ: I didn't take her money. I put it all back. Here. *(HE takes out some money.)* You can leave him with me when you go shopping.

—You don't trust me. I don't blame you.

35

THE HAVE-LITTLE

LILLIAN: You better go now.

JOSÉ: I just got here. Have another little drink with me.

LILLIAN: No, pa. It's time for you to go. I gotta put Joey to bed.

JOSÉ: He's sleeping already.

LILLIAN: I have to put him in his bed.

JOSÉ: Okay..but you come see me again. I'm always here except on Monday and Tuesday. That's when I work.

LILLIAN: That's good, Pa. You go home. *(Taking JOEY)* Goodbye, now. *(HE pours himself another drink)* You don't change, do you?

JOSÉ: Why should I? Nuffin else does.

LILLIAN: *(Pause; with a small smile)* Joey's gonna paint pictures like this one. *(Pulls out a drawing)* Like this.

JOSÉ: That tree don't got no leaves on it.

LILLIAN: That's okay. It ain't really a tree.

JOSÉ: What's it?

LILLIAN: It's God. I seen him, Pa. Like you used to. There's places where he's everywhere. He comes down waterfalls and he sings in a circle. He's got sweet fruit. And my baby's gonna taste that fruit.

JOSÉ: Baby? *(Remembers)* Yeah...Hercules, right? Yeah. *(Laughs)* he's—he's jus' like me, Lily.

LILLIAN: He ain't one pissy-shit like you. *(SHE fills his tumbler to the brim.)*

JOSÉ: That's my baby girl! *(Pause)* Scratch my arms, baby.

LILLIAN: Pa...

JOSÉ: Use your nails.

LILLIAN: I don' got no more nails.

JOSÉ: Everybody got nails! What you think? You some kind of animal wif no fuckin' nails? What's that? A fish or somefin?

LILLIAN: I'm a turttle, Pa. Like the one you ain't never got me. *(Pause)* You wanna go somewhere, Pa?

JOSÉ: I jus' got here... *(SHE gets a small globe and puts it in front of JOSÉ.)* Oh.

LILLIAN: You first. *(JOSÉ spins the globe and then stops it with a finger.)* New York.

JOSÉ: I hate this game. *(LILLIAN spins it with her eyes closed and*

36

THE HAVE-LITTLE

stops it with a finger.)
LILLIAN: Shit. I always get the fuckin' ocean.
JOSÉ: I like the water.
LILLIAN: You know how ta swim. *(Pause)*
JOSÉ: I saw Saint Martin.
LILLIAN: When?
JOSÉ: Today. Jus' before I got here.
LILLIAN: What was he doing?
JOSÉ: He was holding the Baby Jesus and he said "Don't worry about nuffin. You're gonna get a job."
LILLIAN: Yeah?
JOSÉ: Yeah...in a liquor store.
LILLIAN: There's other places, Pa.
JOSÉ: I know. There's New York and the ocean.
LILLIAN: Go home.
JOSÉ: Don' you get lonely here?
LILLIAN: I like being alone. Then there ain't nobody to make you feel left out. *(Pause)*
JOSÉ: Rub my arms. Please, baby. *(LILLIAN runs her nails lightly across his arms.)* Harder. *(SHE scratches his arms.)*
LILLIAN: Do you remember how Mami smelled? I remember... sweaty and warm and sweet like sugar. But I don't see her face no more...just a smell. I bet she din't smell like that to nobody but me.
(JOSÉ kisses her passionately. She pushes him away, holding onto his hands.)
LILLIAN: Your hands are too skinny, Pa. I can feel all the bones.
JOSÉ: I always loved your hands, Carmen. When I first saw 'em, I first fell in love. They was holding some rosary beads and when you counted off ten more Hail Marys, I wanned to put my ten fingers inside you. I wanned to feel up inside you till I had my hands around your heart. I could always feel your heart down there, Carmen. I wanned to touch your heart.
LILLIAN: I ain't Carmen!
JOSÉ: *(Flinging her across the room)* Then you ain't nuffin to me.
LILLIAN: You're the one that's nuffin. You killed her—you let her die alone. *(HE runs out the door.)*

37

HURLYBURLY
by David Rabe
Hollywood - Present - Eddie (30's) - Darlene (30's)

Eddie - A casting agent
Darlene - Eddie's roommate's lover

This play deals with the lives of casting agents and roommates
Eddie and Mickey. In this scene, Mickey and Darlene are
presently involved. However, Mickey has given Eddie and
Darlene permission to act upon their mutual attraction. They are
thrilled, but each wants to make sure the other understands that
there are no strings attached.

EDDIE *(Pacing toward the door as if in awe of Mickey)*: Where the
hell did he come up with the... I mean, clarity to do that?
DARLENE: That wasn't clarity.
EDDIE *(Turning toward Darlene, he perches on the couch arm)*: No,
no, I mean, it wasn't clarity. But he had to HAVE clarity.
DARLENE: I don't know what it was. Generosity?
EDDIE: Whatever it was, you don't see it very often. I don't expect
that from Mickey, I mean, that kind of thing.
DARLENE: Who expects that from anybody? We're all so all over
the place.
EDDIE: Self-absorbed.
DARLENE: And distracted. I'm distracted by everything. I mean,
I'm almost always distracted, aren't you?
EDDIE: Absolutely.
DARLENE: Everything is always distracting me from everything else.
EDDIE: Everything is very distracting, but what I've really noticed is
that mainly, the thing I'm most distracted by is myself. I mean, I'm my
own major distraction, trying to get it together, to get my head together,
my act together.
DARLENE: Our little minds just buzzzzzzzz! What do they think
they're doing?
EDDIE: However Mickey managed to get through it, though, I know
one thing—I'm glad he did.
DARLENE: Are you really?
EDDIE: I really missed you. It was amazing. That was probably it—

he got his clue from the fact that I never shut up about you. I think I was driving him crazy. How do you feel?

DARLENE: Great. I think I was, you know, into some form of obsession about you, too, some form of mental loop. I feel scared is what I feel. Good, too. I feel good, but mainly scared.

EDDIE: I'm scared.

DARLENE: I mean, a year ago, I was a basket case. If we had met a year ago, I wouldn't have had a prayer.

EDDIE: Me, too. A year ago, I was nuts. And I still have all kinds of things to think through. Stuff coming up, I have to think it through.

DARLENE: Me, too.

EDDIE: And by thinking, I don't mean just some ethereal mental thing either, but being with people is part of it, being with you is part of the thinking, that's how I'm doing the thinking, but I just have to go slow, there's a lot of scar tissue.

DARLENE: There's no rush, Eddie.

EDDIE: I don't want to rush.

DARLENE: I don't want to rush.

EDDIE: I can't rush. I'll panic. If I rush, I'll panic.

DARLENE: We'll just have to keep our hearts open, as best we can.

EDDIE: No pressure.

DARLENE: And no guilt, okay?

EDDIE: No guilt.

DARLENE: We don't want any guilt. I mean, I'm going to be out of town a lot. We both have our lives.

EDDIE: We just have to keep our options open.

DARLENE: And our hearts, okay?

EDDIE: I mean, the right attitude...

DARLENE: Exactly. If we have the right attitude...

EDDIE: Attitude is so important. And by attitude I don't mean just attitude either, but I mean real emotional space.

DARLENE: We both need space.

EDDIE: And time. We have to have time.

DARLENE: Right. So we can just take the time to allow the emotional space for things to grow and work themselves out.

EDDIE: So you wanna to fuck?

IS HE STILL DEAD?
by Donald Freed
A hotel in France - 1940 - James Joyce (58) - Nora Joyce (50's)

James Joyce - An author
Nora Joyce - James Joyce's wife

Two months before his death, James Joyce and his wife, Nora plan a Christmas party for their son.

JOYCE: *(He kicks at an open trunk.)* Yes, we'll have a Christmas party—for the boy.
NORA: *(More packing)* We'll have it in Zurich, then.
JOYCE: Wherever we have it. —And champagne.
NORA: For "the boy"? —There, now *(JOYCE is wearing down again. NORA tries to keep his mood up. Continuing)* Sure, we'll lay something on, no matter where. The boy's mad for his sweets.
JOYCE: Your mother was a born cook.
NORA: Sure, we all are. We learned how over an open turf fire back in the Stone Age. *(She returns to her cooking.)*
JOYCE: ...What would he fancy, the boy?
NORA: You tell me.
JOYCE: Ah, well, there's your rhubarb pudding with the meringue topping...
NORA: Oh, aye, and the baked apples wrapped in pastry. *(JOYCE is enjoying a pang of hunger. He drifts over to observe NORA's culinary efforts.)*
JOYCE: Mm... Pudding cake...
NORA: Mm... Stand there.
JOYCE; What's that?
NORA: Syrup of figs.
JOYCE; Who's it for?
NORA: You.
JOYCE: No.
NORA: It is. It'll wash you out.
JOYCE: Well... Damson jam, do you think? For the Christmas breakfast.

IS HE STILL DEAD?

NORA: Now, where would I—

JOYCE: And barm bracks.

NORA: Barm bracks?

JOYCE: Definately.

NORA: Is it Hallowe'en you're talking about or Christmas?

JOYCE: Definately. With a ring inside for Stephen.

NORA: For the boy.

JOYCE: Yes.

NORA: *(Laughs)* When you put one on as a wedding ring—I could've killed you—blatherin' that you only wore it because it "eased" your hand from "the writer's cramp."

JOYCE: *(Dreaming and drifting)* ...Rice pudding and tarts... And treacle bread...

NORA: Stand over there, will ye?

JOYCE: What's that?

NORA: Fillet of salmon.

JOYCE: Mm.

NORA: Very mild...

JOYCE: The boy's mad for "boxty".

NORA: Mm.

JOYCE: Your mother made it the best.

"Boxty on the griddle, boxty in the pan,

If you don't eat boxty you'll never get a man."

NORA: She had a "secret Galwegian recipe."

JOYCE: What?

NORA: Sit down till I'm through. —Mm? Oh, umm, let's see, She'd take the raw potatoes; grate 'em in muslin cloth; mix 'em with flour; salt 'em; shape 'em into dumplings—move aside will ye, Jim?—boil 'em—

JOYCE: The dumplings?

NORA: Sweet Grace above—the dumplings. Boil 'em in a big pot till they were lovely gray and slimy; then slice 'em thin and fry 'em with eggs...

JOYCE: Then eat 'em.

NORA: *(A burst of laughter)* Yes! —Here, dry your lips, sure, you're droolin'.

JOYCE: Annie Barnacle's "secret recipe."

NORA: Mm.

JOYCE: *(Pause)* "Her portrait has passed." *(NORA, too, remembers the phrase from The Portrait of the Artist.)*

JOYCE: *(Continuing, pause)* What else?

NORA: What else what?

JOYCE: What else did we used to eat? —Sherry trifle? Pickled pigs trotters?

NORA: Is it your memory that's goin', now? Let me alone and they'll be back within the hour and you'll have your dinner. For a thin man, you're a terrible glutton.

JOYCE: My mother, now, put currants in her barm bracks—

NORA: No, now, let's talk about Zurich and Christmas and not Ireland and the *(Sings)* "dear dead days beyond recall," forty years and more ago. Please.

JOYCE: *(Sings a pure phrase)* "Just a song at twilight..."

NORA: *(Pause)* They'll be back any time, now.

JOYCE: If he's taken the boy into the hotel bar, I'll cut him out of my will as I would and "embossed carbuncle!"

NORA: *(Laughs)* Your will? Is it King Lear you are, now—

JOYCE: My son is a drunkard. When he has the money. Full stop. Don't argue with me. You're as blind when it comes to him as I am when I try to see the proofs of my—

NORA: As you are—when it comes to Lucia!

JOYCE: That's enough, then.

NORA: She had a glee eye as a child, but, no, you told people that she "looked like Norma Shearer"!

JOYCE: *(Pause)* I intend to dine in the hotel restaurant today, for my stomach's sake.

NORA: Will you listen—the man will say anything at all.

JOYCE: I want a piece of red meat, I tell you—I'm that bored.

NORA: You think that you're "bored"?! *(She resumes packing.)*

JOYCE: *(Pause)* You've sex on your mind—night and day.

NORA: In the mind, not on it, in it. Sex in the mind and in the book—not the bed, the book. A book so dirty that in America it drove them into the streets to fornicate. Ahh, but that's "Literature." *(Slamming cases)*

JOYCE: Philistine.

NORA: Irishman!

JOYCE: Prude.

NORA: Panderer.

JOYCE: Peasant. Puritan.

NOAR: Pervert.

JOYCE: Censor.

NORA: Pornographer.

JOYCE: Critic!

NORA: No one can call me that! *(She throws a utensil.)* You drunken sleeveen.

JOYCE: I've a drink taken—

NORA: —Hah! A bucketful.

JOYCE: —A sup taken in my time—

NORA: —Ha-ha! You've drunk the Liffey in your time!

JOYCE: —But I-am-not-a-drunk!

NORA: You'll do till the genuine article comes along!

NORA: Oh, no, you're not! The only place you're goin' is Zurich!

(NORA blocks his way. JOYCE puts on his hat and tries to take off his dressing gown but NORA wrestles him to a stand still. Both shout at each other at the same time, wearing their voices down to a croaking melody. NORA's pace is staccato, with no pause, while JOYCE speaks in short bursts, breathing hard.)

NORA:	JOYCE:
I'll muder ye, ye cursagod,	How dare you? Get away and
you. Ye little shoneen,	get out. I take the odd drop
you. Ye big boozer, you.	as a "medicament" and you
You ignorant gombeen,	pounce on me like the bag of
you—Raise your hand to me,	cats that you are. —Let
will you, you dirty jackeen,	go! I'll have a glass of
you yahoo, you. Satan	porter before the mid day
(pronounced satin), get ye	meal, if I fancy it.

IS HE STILL DEAD?

behind me. With your
Paddy whiskey and your cork
gin and your Dutch
courage—It's a matter for
the police—I'll have your
grandson baptized, and have
him christened—I'm goin'
for the priest now—
You're not a writer at all,
you used everybody—used
your own family—
put 'em in your dirty
book—
used me, inside and out,
early and late...
...girl and woman—used me,
with no shame and no
thanks!—It's a matter
for the police now, I'm
going to have you LOCKED UP
with Lucia—

(Coughing)
It's because I'm in pain!
You've no mercy. You're a
peasant and you've no idea
the comfort in a ball of
hot malt when you're in pain.
(He pants, recovers, resumes.)
I'll have a small Irish and
Apollinairis! *(with a
flourish, as Falstaff)*

"Bring me a bottle of sack
and put a cheeze in't!"
I'll go out on the road, I
tell you, like Tolstoy—
I'll walk across Europe
with my child, my daughter—
like Tolstoy, like Lear!

*(They have run down. He collapses in her arms. They have heard and
hurt each other. He quotes Lear; her head falls on his chest. She
sighs, "Jim, ah, Jim.")*

44

KEY EXCHANGE
by Kevin Wade
Central Park, NYC - Present - Lisa (30's) - Philip (30's)

Lisa - A woman looking for a commitment from her lover
Philip - Lisa's lover

Lisa and Philip have a relationship that she would very much
like to make permanent. Here, they quarrel about their situation
and the future.

*(Philip is lying on his stomach. Lisa straddles him, massaging his
shoulders and back.)*
PHILIP: Yes.
LISA: There?
PHILIP: Yes. Ah.
LISA: You've got a big knot here. *(Presses a spot)* Feel it?
PHILIP: Ouch! Easy. Just massage it a little, huh? You don't have
to squash it.
LISA: Relax. Breathe deep. Stop resisting. *(She continues kneading
his back. Philip breathes loudly)* It's like armor.
PHILIP: I've got a strong back.
LISA: You've also got a lot of tension. *(Pressing a spot)* That's from
tension.
PHILIP: *(Wincing)* Ow. Christ.
LISA: Relax.
PHILIP: I'm relaxed already.
LIDA: Breathe.
PHILIP: I'm breathing.
LISA: It's like golf balls. You're carrying a lot of stuff back here.
PHILIP: It's pure energy. I store it back there. *(Winces)* Ah, that's
enough. That's good. Thanks.
LISA: *(Getting up)* Fine. Be tense.
PHILIP: *(Sitting up and rubbing his shoulder)* It takes years to build
up knots like that. They don't just come undone in a few minutes.
(Turns to her) Thank you.
LISA: You're welcome.

45

KEY EXCHANGE

PHILIP: Want me to do you?

LISA: Would you?

PHILIP: No. Yes. Lie down.

LISA: My legs could use some work. *(Lisa lies down on her back. Philip kneels beside her. He starts with her calves)*

PHILIP: How's that?

LISA: That's good. *(He continues on past her knees and to her thighs)* Oh yeah. There. That's it, ah yes. *(Philip kneads a little harder. Lisa starts laughing)* Oh don't tickles oh ah-ha eow stop it that tickles. *(He stops, starts again gently)* Oh God. Oh. You shouldn't do that. It shocks the muscles when you do that.

PHILIP: You can't shock these thighs. They've seen it all. *(He leans over, talking to her legs)* Right, you guys? That night docked outside Corfu? The moon, the stars, the retsina, the waves lapping at the hull, that Turkish tanker crew lapping at the two of you. *(Lisa laughs. Philip continues gently massaging her thighs. This goes on for a few moments)*

LISA: I'm meeting my father and his wife for dinner tonight.

PHILIP: That's nice. Where are you eating?

LISA: Tavern on the Green.

PHILIP: Delicious.

LISA: You're invited.

PHILIP: Oh.

LISA: I'd like you to come.

PHILIP: *(after a moment)* I don't think so.

LISA: Why not?

PHILIP: I just wouldn't feel comfortable. Not yet. *(He ends the massage and sits back)*

LISA: Everyone feels comfortable with my father. And he really wants to meet you. You'll like him, Philip. He's a big mystery fan too. When I was a kid, he used to read me to sleep with Raymond Chandler stories.

PHILIP: Really?

LISA: Yeah. He'd do Bogart and imitate a saxophone and everything.

PHILIP: That's great. *(Pause)* I can't come.

KEY EXCHANGE

LISA: Why not?

PHILIP: I just can't.

LISA: That's not an answer.

PHILIP: It'll have to do, all right?

LISA: No, not all right?

PHILIP: I can't come because he's your father and he'll know I'm screwing his daughter.

LISA: That's ridiculous.

PHILIP: It's not ridiculous. It's the nut of the situation.

LISA: He doesn't care about that. I'm not his little girl anymore.

PHILIP: He cares, believe me. There will come a point when it will hit him, he'll realize that this guy inhaling the endive across the table is doing his only daughter every which way, and it'll grab his gut, and he'll try to be casual, maybe shoot me a little smile and a knowing wink, and I'll catch it and try to look worthy, but in our hearts we'll both know what's going on.

LISA: That's not true.

PHILIP: It's the primal paternal reaction.

LISA: It's a load of baloney.

PHILIP: You don't understand.

LISA: (After a moment) I think I do understand. It's like the keys, isn't it?

PHILIP: What?

LISA: Exchanging our keys. And the Tampax in your bathroom closet. And all the other times you take a little thing and blow it up and look into the future and see yourself stuck. (Imitating him) So say I go eat with you and your father. Then you know what happens? I'll tell you what happens. Next thing, you're getting chummy with my parents. Then it's ball games with your old man. Then Thanksgiving with my folks, you and my mother are in the big cahoots, and Uncle Whoever is wanting to know if we've set a fucking date yet...

PHILIP: STOP IT!

LISA: Well isn't that it, Philip?

PHILIP: Stop pushing me.

LISA: Pushing you? Jesus, I ask you out for a dinner and you make

47

it sound like the last supper.

PHILIP: No, you made it sound like that. You stuffed all those words in my mouth, you do that so you can make me wrong.

LISA: You hear the same spiel enough, Philip, you get a feel for when it's coming.

PHILIP: That's good. Why should I come to dinner? You don't need me, you could just keep switching seats and be both of us, you know so fucking much.

LISA: What are you so scared of?

PHILIP: Christ, Lisa, come on.

LISA: No, Philip, you come on.

PHILIP: Not wanting to meet your father tonight doesn't make me scared.

LISA: Then I don't know what it is, but it's something. I see it when you've had a few drinks, or when we're making love, and you'll say I love you, and damnit you mean it, and then you'll do a thing with your eyes, a funny little frown, and then you cut off, you order another drink, or roll over and make a joke and get out of bed. Anything you have to go out on a limb for, you tag a disclaimer on it and wiggle away. It makes me feel like shit.

PHILIP: Lisa, I can't just snap my fingers and be where you want me to be. I've got my own pace, it doesn't pop change like...

LISA: Pace is a lot of bull. You either want me or you don't. This isn't a bicycle race, you're not pacing yourself in a pack. This is you and me. *(Pause)* I can't do this anymore. I'm tired of holding myself back. And I deserve better than this. I'm smart and pretty and funny and there are a lot of guys, good men, who would be proud to have me show them off to my father, and who would be pleased as punch to have a key to my apartment, and yes even happy to keep a box of Tampax in the bathroom closet. *(She gets her knapsack and pulls it on.)*

PHILIP: Lisa, please, don't go.

LISA: I have to go.

PHILIP: I love you. I do. I'm sorry I'm such a fuck up.

LISA: I'm sorry too, Philip.

KEY EXCHANGE

PHILIP: I'll come to dinner tonight. I'd like to.

LISA: Don't do that.

PHILIP: I'll meet your father.

LISA: Don't. Not now. It's forced, I don't want it forced. No more pulling teeth. Ums and buts and well all rights.

(Michael enters, stage left. They don't notice him. He is stooped over, holding his bicycle and catching his breath)

LISA: No more excuses. About dinner with my father, about the importance of screwing around, about your goddamn pace. I'm sick of fighting you every inch of the way.

KURU
by Josh Manheimer
Papua, New Guinea - 1950's - Dr. Roman (30's) - Mary Lou (30's)

Dr. Arthur Roman - A distinguished physician
Mary Lou Anderson - A blonde cooking instructor from Iowa

Dr. Roman has been in the New Guinea jungle for two years, trying to find a cure for Kuru, a fatal disease that afflicts the natives. To his surprise, his fiancee, Mary Lou, arrives from Iowa. They have not spoken to each other since he left the States.

DR. ROMAN: Mary Lou. I'm doing my best to get across to you, these people play Life by different rules. You are going to have to See a little differently if you are to be helpful to my research. You are going to have to accept Alternative Points of View.

MARY LOU: Don't lecture to me Arthur. You always treat me like I'm some lower form of life. An intern or something. I didn't travel half-way around the world to play red light green light. Don't be so sure, I'm as inflexible as you think. I watched a lot of National Geographic specials in the past couple a years. I'm not as puffed up as you are about my intelligence. When daddy flipped the tractor, I went to work and now run the best cooking class in Iowa. I've know what adversity means even though I may not be able to spell it. There is not much you can say that will shock me at this point.

DR. ROMAN: Hmmm.

MARY LOU: Try me.

DR. ROMAN: Well, first, you cannot leave. How you got here without getting killed, I cannot fathom. The clinic in Port Moresby sends a patrol in once every three months to bring me supplies. They just left here last week.

MARY LOU: I'm still standing.

DR. ROMAN: Second. As you have just witnessed, all the women are dying of a mysterious slow fatal degenerative brain disease. At the start you lose your balance and smile stupidly. There is nothing funny about it. Excitement of any sort causes progressive locomotor ataxia with

50

uncontrollable myoclonic jerks.

MARY LOU: Talk like a human being.

DR. ROMAN: Your mind remains completely lucid while you lose all control of your limbs. You watch helplessly as your body is taken over by some Other Force which you cannot control. Until I find the cure, nothing can be done.

MARY LOU: Oh.

DR. ROMAN: Soon, after you are no longer able to stand, swallowing becomes impossible. If you don't die of starvation, you are left indoors where you become so despondent you roll into the fire pit and are fatally burned. Unfortunately, I'm no closer to a solution then when I left you.

MARY LOU: Go on.

DR. ROMAN: Third. This will be especially difficult. It is no reflection on you. But to be accepted. To perform my research. To get inside, if you will. I have had to make some accommodations. I have had to Play By Their Rules. I have been given, and I accepted, a Mai Mai.

MARY LOU: What?

DR. ROMAN: A Mai Mai. A mate. The chief has very graciously given me his daughter.

MARY LOU: He gave you his daughter. What the hell does that mean?

DR. ROMAN: I have a wife.

MARY LOU: A wife?

DR. ROMAN: Yes.

MARY LOU: You're married?

DR. ROMAN: Yes.

MARY LOU: You married someone else?

DR. ROMAN: Yes.

MARY LOU: You're not serious?

DR. ROMAN: I'm afraid so.

MARY LOU: You're not marrying me?

DR. ROMAN: And there's more.

MARY LOU: More?

KURU

DR. ROMAN: When I married her, she was thirteen.

MARY LOU: Thirteen?

DR. ROMAN: Yes.

MARY LOU: What? You married a thirteen-year-old?

DR. ROMAN: That's correct.

MARY LOU: Are you some kind of pervert?

DR. ROMAN: It's not unusual in this culture...

MARY LOU: I don't feel well.

DR. ROMAN: ...for an adult to take—

MARY LOU: —shut up for a minute, will you.

DR. ROMAN: I was trying to explain...

MARY LOU: Two years ago you made a mortal vow to me. You think you can just go away to some jungle and poof it disappears. Was I some kind of experiment? How does the heart look when it's been put through your Vegematic?

DR. ROMAN: But...

MARY LOU: Shut up and let me talk. Your marriage will not stand up in any court. What do I look like? Do you know how far I traveled to get here? What I had to sell to raise the money for airfare? The humiliation of telling people your letters were taken by pirates in some shipwreck. I lugged my wedding dress halfway around the world to make sure you liked it. Why? Why? Why? Why? Why? *(She hits him)*

DR. ROMAN: Mary Lou...please...

MARY LOU: I'm going to Take You To The Cleaners. I don't know how. But kiss your precious career goodbye. Get your stuff out of here. I get the hut. I want you gone. Now. Bye. Over. I'm ending it. Not you. Take your wife with you. I'm leaving tomorrow. I don't care if I get killed. It'll be your fault. I don't know where I'm going, I gotta go.

DR. ROMAN: I knew you were not going to take this well. It must be a deep and bitter blow. Somewhere in your heart, you must have known my ambition was far too great to practice medicine in Beaver City.

MARY LOU: All I know it wasn't too big for you to get misty-eyed that Christmas and ask for my hand in the most sacred act one human can do to another. Was I just the farmer's daughter? You could have skipped the—

DR. ROMAN: —I was unschooled.

MARY LOU: Well, that's the first time you've ever admitted that. I knew you were a Man. And that meant you had it in you to be evil, cruel, heartless, selfish, and conceited. But your big words diverted me. *(Pause)* What if we didn't stay in Beaver City? I came all the way here. I could stay with you here. We could get married and live on some island somewhere. The three of us.

DR. ROMAN: Mary Lou. Let's look at the situation clinically.

MARY LOU: No! Damn you! I don't want to look at it clinically. You coward! You Man! You Wimp! You little piece of dog turd!

DR. ROMAN: Mary Lou. Let's try to put aside our enmities and overcome this initial obstacle.

MARY LOU: You goat's ass! You ugly dwarf! You piece of mashed gore!

DR. ROMAN: Perhaps we can roll up our sleeves together...

MARY LOU: You balding oafish pig-faced eggplant!

DR. ROMAN: *(Protecting himself with a native shield)* MARY LOU!

MARY LOU: What?

DR. ROMAN: Please, of course there is always the chance I may wish to reconsider. One never knows what can happen. Perhaps if we work together for a while. There is much to be done...

MARY LOU: Spit it out, blow fish. I got a train to catch.

DR. ROMAN: Whether you or I like it, we are stuck here with each other. There's much work to be done. Great achievements to conquer. Awards to be won. Let's put our shoulders into it, yes? Madame and Louis Pasteur. Perhaps something between us will rekindle...

MARY LOU: There's something to pin my life on.

DR. ROMAN: The natives believe you are a goddess. They believe you have fallen from the sky to save them. Never in your life will you face such an experience. They've slaughtered a herd of pigs for you. They worship you. You are the Homecoming Queen. They will believe whatever you tell them. Dozens of men will kiss your feet.

KURU

They'll rub your body with pig grease. Will you please stay and accept this new position?

MARY LOU: What about your wife?

DR. ROMAN: She'll have to understand.

MARY LOU: What are my alternatives?

DR. ROMAN: You can return through three-hundred miles of the deepest darkest jungle on earth. If the wart hogs don't gore you, and the leeches don't suck all your blood, then cannibals will surely peel the skin from your flesh while you are still alive.

MARY LOU: This pig party they're throwing for me. What should I wear?

DR. ROMAN: As little as possible.

LARGO DESOLATO
by Vaclav Havel
English version by Tom Stoppard
Leopold's living room - Present - Leopold (40-50) - Marguerite (20's)

Leopold - A troubled intellectual
Marguerite - Leopold's young admirer

Confounded by life's complexities, Marguerite decides to pay a
visit to her favorite philosopher in hopes that the well-known
author can help her to sort things out. Leopold turns out to be
very different than what she expected, however, and Marguerite
finds that she is in a position to offer him the help that she had
desired for herself.

*(The music fades as the curtain rises. There is no one on the stage.
The bathroom door is open. There is the sound of running water and
of LEOPOLD gasping. There is a short pause. Then the bell rings.
The sound of water stops and LEOPOLD runs out of the bathroom. He
was obviously having a shower. He is wet and is covered only by a
towel wrapped round his waist. He runs to the main door, looks
through the peep-hole, is taken aback, hesitates a moment and then
opens the door. MARGUERITE enters.)*

MARGUERITE: Good evening—
LEOPOLD: *(A bit nonplussed)* Good evening— *(Short pause.)*
MARGUERITE: Professor Nettles?
LEOPOLD: Yes— *(Short pause.)*
MARGUERITE: Sorry to disturb you—
LEOPOLD: You're not disturbing me—
MARGUERITE: I won't hold you up for long—
LEOPOLD: I've got time— *(Short pause.)*
MARGUERITE: My name's Marguerite. I'm a student of
philosophy—
LEOPOLD: At the university or a private student?
MARGUERITE: Both— *(MARGUERITE walks to the middle of the
room and looks round uncertainly. LEOPOLD closes the door. A short
pause.)*

LARGO DESOLATO

LEOPOLD: Sit down—

MARGUERITE: Thank you— *(MARGUERITE sits down shyly on the edge of the sofa.)*

LEOPOLD: Would you like some rum?

MARGUERITE: No—thank you—I'm not used to rum—

LEOPOLD: One glass won't do you any harm— *(LEOPOLD pours some rum into the glass which has remained on the table.)*

MARGUERITE: Well, thank you— *(MARGUERITE takes a very small sip and winces.)*

LEOPOLD: Not bad is it?

MARGUERITE: No— *(Awkward pause.)* You'll catch cold.

LEOPOLD: Ah yes, of course— *(LEOPOLD goes quickly into the bathroom and comes back in a moment wearing a dressing gown under which he is naked. He sits down on the sofa next to MARGUERITE and smiles at her. MARGUERITE smiles back. There is a longer awkward pause.)*

MARGUERITE: I know your work—

LEOPOLD: Really? Which?

MARGUERITE: *Phenomenology of Responsibility, Love and Nothingness, Ontology of the Human Self—*

LEOPOLD: You've read all those?

MARGUERITE: Several times—

LEOPOLD: Well, I am impressed— *(Pause.)*

MARGUERITE: I hear *Ontology of the Human Self* got you into trouble—

LEOPOLD: It's because of that I'm supposed to go there—

MARGUERITE: What—straight there? How come?

LEOPOLD: Paragraph 511—intellectual hooliganism—

MARGUERITE: That's awful!

LEOPOLD: That's the sort of world we're living in—

MARGUERITE: For such beautiful thoughts!

LEOPOLD: Apparently someone didn't think they were so beautiful—

MARGUERITE: And is it definite?

LEOPOLD: I could get out of it by denying that I wrote it—

MARGUERITE: Is that what they're offering you?

LARGO DESOLATO

LEOPOLD: Yes—

MARGUERITE: They're disgusting! *(Pause. MARGUERITE takes a sip and winces. LEOPOLD promptly fills up her glass.)* Your essays have given me a great deal of—

LEOPOLD: Yes? I'm so glad—

MARGUERITE: It's because of them that I became interested in philosophy—

LEOPOLD: Really?

MARGUERITE: Somehow they opened my eyes—

LEOPOLD: You're exaggerating—

MARGUERITE: Really—

LEOPOLD: Have another drink— *(MARGUERITE has a drink and winces. LEOPOLD promptly refills her glass. Awkward pause.)*

MARGUERITE: Are you writing anything?

LEOPOLD: I'm trying to—

MARGUERITE: Could you tell me—excuse my curiosity—could you tell me what you're writing?

LEOPOLD: I'm trying to think about love as a dimension of being—

MARGUERITE: You touched on that a little in the second chapter of *Love and Nothingness*—

LEOPOLD: That's right— *(Awkward pause.)*

MARGUERITE: Professor—

LEOPOLD: Yes, Marguerite?

MARGUERITE: I wouldn't dare trouble you—

LEOPLOD: You're not troubling me at all! On the contrary—I'm very pleased to have met you—

MARGUERITE: If it wasn't for the fact that I'm sure you're the only one who can help me—

LEOPOLD: What's the matter?

MARGUERITE: It's going to sound silly—

LEOPOLD: You can tell me!

MARGUERITE: I'm suddenly embarrassed—

LEOPOLD: But why, there's no need— *(MARGUERITE has a drink and winces. LEOPOLD promptly refills her glass. Short pause.)*

MARGUERITE: Where should I begin? I just don't know what to

do—

LEOPOLD: In your studies?

MARGUERITE: In my life—

LEOPOLD: In your life?

MARGUERITE: I find everything so stifling—all those hopeless faces in the bus queues—the endless hue and cry in the streets—people twisted out of shape in their offices and everywhere else—the general misery of life—forgive me, I know it's silly, you don't even know me—but I didn't know anyone else I could turn to—

LEOPOLD: I'm delighted that you should confide in me—

MARGUERITE: I don't get on with my parents—they're middle class types who are always watching TV—I've no boyfriend—the other students seem terribly superficial—

LEOPOLD: I know what you mean—

MARGUERITE: You're not angry?

LEOPOLD: Why do you make excuses for yourself all the time? What greater satisfaction could there be for a philosopher than to receive a visit from a reader in mid-crisis about the meaning of life?

MARGUERITE: I know that you can't solve my problem for me—

LEOPOLD: You're right in the sense that the meaning of life is not something which one can summarize or verbalize one way or the other and then hand over like a piece of information—it's not an object, it's more like an elusive spiritual state—and the more one needs it the more elusive it becomes—

MARGUERITE: Yes, yes, that's exactly—

LEOPOLD: On the other hand there is the fact—as I've already tried to show in *Ontology of the Human Self*—that there's a certain non-verbal, existential space in which—and only in which—once can get hold of something through experiencing the presence of another person—

MARGUERITE: Forgive me, it's exactly that part—it's from chapter four—which made me decide to come and see you—

LEOPOLD: There you are! But I wouldn't like to raise your hopes unduly, because the fact that I'm meditating on this subject doesn't automatically mean that I am myself capable of creating such a space—

LARGO DESOLATO

MARGUERITE: But you've been creating it for ages—by talking to me at all—by understanding me—forgive me, I'm probably already a bit tipsy—

LEOPOLD: Not at all! Drink up— *(MARGUERITE takes a drink and winces. LEOPOLD promptly fills up her glass.)*

LEOPOLD: I'll tell you something, Marguerite—honesty deserves honesty: if I am able to understand you then it is mainly because I'm in a similar or perhaps even worse situation than you—

MARGUERITE: You? I can't believe it! You know so much—you've achieved so much—you're so wise—

LEOPOLD: That guarantees nothing—

MARGUERITE: I'm only a silly girl, but you—

LEOPOLD: You're not silly—

MARGUERITE: I am, I know it—

LEOPOLD: You're clever, Marguerite—and not only that, you're beautiful—

MARGUERITE: Me? Well, whatever next—

LEOPOLD: I'll be quite frank with you, Marguerite: I'm in a very bad way—

MARGUERITE: I know life has been hard on you but you seem so strong—

LEOPOLD: Alas, that's only appearance. In reality I've had the feeling for some time now that something is collapsing inside me—as if an axis holding me together has started to break—the ground crumbling under my feet—I lack a fixed point from which everything inside me could grow and develop—I get the feeling sometimes that I'm not really doing anything except listening helplessly to the time going by. Gone is the perspective I once had—my humour—my industry and persistence—the pointedness of my observations—

MARGUERITE: How beautifully you put it—

LEOPOLD: You should have known me before! It's all gone, my irony, my self-irony, my capacity for enthusiasm, for emotional involvement, for commitment, even for sacrifice! This might disappoint you, Marguerite, but for a long time I haven't been the person that you obviously take me for! Basically I'm a tired, dried out,

59

broken man—

MARGUERITE: You mustn't speak like that, Professor! You're too hard on yourself! But even if it were all true the very fact that you are reflecting upon your situatin shows that all is not lost—

LEOPOLD: You're good to me, Marguerite! And please don't call me professor, it sounds so formal! Why aren't you drinking? *(MARGUERITE has a drink and winces. LEOPOLD promptly fills up her glass. Short pause.)*

MARGUERITE: So many people think so highly of you! Doesn't that alone give you strength?

LEOPOLD: On the contrary! I often say to myself how wonderful it was when nobody was interested in me—when nobody expected anything from me and nobody was urging me to do things—I used to browse around the second-hand bookshops—studying modern philosophers at my leisure—spending the nights making notes from their works—taking walks in the parks and meditating—

MARGUERITE: But it's thanks to all that you are what you are today-

LEOPOLD: That's true, but it's also true that I've taken upon myself a heavier burden than I'm able to bear—

MARGUERITE: Leopold, I believe that you will win through!

LEOPOLD: I have a feeling that my only way out is to accept a term there—somewhere far away from my nearest and dearest—and put my humble trust in a higher will, to give me the chance to atone for my guilt—to lose my apathy and regain my pride—and as a nameless cog in a giant machine to purify myself—thus and only thus—If I manage to drain the bitter cup with dignity—I can get back—perhaps something of my lost human integrity—renew the hope inside me—reconstitute myself emotionally—open the door to a new life—

MARGUERITE: *(Shouts)* But Leopold!

LEOPOLD: Yes?

MARGUERITE: *(Excitedly)* Don't you see that the punishment is deeply unjust and if you try—however honourably—to turn it into a purifying experience you'd just be agreeing with it and so prostrating yourself before it. And what's more, by giving it this so-called meaning you're hiding from yourself the fact that you're clinging to it

60

as a kind of escape from your life, a way out of your problems. But however far they send you, punishment won't solve what you can't solve yourself! Don't you understand that you've done nothing and so there is nothing to atone! You're innocent!

LEOPOLD: Oh, Marguerite—why didn't I meet you before it was too late? *(LEOPOLD takes hold of her hands and kisses them. MARGUERITE is embarrassed. LEOPOLD holds her hands. She drops her eyes. Long pause)*

MARGUERITE: *(Whispering)* Leopold—

LEOPOLD: Yes—

MARGUERITE: Do you love anybody?

LEOPOLD: Ah, my dear girl, I really don't know if I'm capable of love—

MARGUERITE: Don't tell me that you've never felt anything towards a woman—

LEOPOLD: Nervousness—more with some, less with others—

MARGUERITE: You need love! Mad passionate true love! Didn't you yourself write in *Phenomenology of Responsibility* that a person who doesn't love doesn't exist? Only love will give you the strength to stand up to them!

LEOPOLD: That's easy for you to say, Marguerite, but where would one find it? *(MARGUERITE takes a quick drink, winces and quietly blurts out.)*

MARGUERITE: With me!

LEOPOLD: What? You?

MARGUERITE: *(Excited)* Yes! You have given back the meaning to my life, which is to give you the meaning back to yours! I'll save you! *(LEOPOLD strokes her hair.)*

LEOPOLD: You're wonderful, Marguerite! But I can't allow you to throw your life away on someone as worthless as myself.

MARGUERITE: On the contrary I would be fulfilling my life!

LEOPOLD: Apart from the fact that I'm an old man—

MARGUERITE: That's nonsense! I've made up my mind—

LEOPOLD: If I'd known it would come to this I'd never have told you my problems—

61

LARGO DESOLATO

MARGUERITE: Thank goodness you did! I'll give you back strength—courage—self-confidence—joy—appetite for life! I'll bring your failing heart back to life! I know you're capable of love! How else could you have written those things! I'll bring you back to life and at the same time back to philosophy! *(LEOPOLD takes hold of MARGUERITE's arms and for a moment looks deeply into her eyes and then begins to kiss her rapidly over her face and neck.)*
MARGUERITE: Ah—Leopold—ah—I love you—I love your thoughts and your words—you awoke my love a long time ago without knowing it—without my knowing it—and now I'll awaken love in you!

LES LIAISONS DANGEREUSES
by Christopher Hampton
Paris - 1780's - Merteuil (30's) - Valmont (30's)

Merteuil - A respectable widow of considerable means
Valmont - A charming and calculating man

Valmont and his cohort, Merteuil, play games of sexual intrigue
and conquest. Here, Valmont returns to Merteuil after having
accepted her challenge to brutally end his relationship with his
beloved Tourvel.

*(About a week later. A December evening in MME DE MERTEUIL's
salon. MERTEUIL sits at a small escritoire, writing. After a time
VALMONT appears in the doorway, once again unannounced.
MERTEUIL, with her back to the door, doesn't see him, but as he
approaches, she looks up, hearing a footstep, and speaks without
turning round.)*

MERTEUIL: Is that you? You're early.

VALMONT: Am I? *(MERTEUIL spins around, startled; to be greeted
with an ironic bow from VALMONT.)* I wanted to ask you: that story
you told me, how did it end?

MERTEUIL: I'm not sure I know what you mean.

VALMONT: Well, once this friend of yours had taken the advice of
his lady-friend, did she take him back?

MERTEUIL: Am I to understand...?

VALMONT: The day after our last meeting, I broke with Madame de
Tourvel. On the grounds that it was beyond my control. *(A slow smile
of great satisfaction spreads across MERTEUIL's face.)*

MERTEUIL: You didn't

VALMONT: I certainly did.

MERTEUIL: Seriously?

VALMONT: On my honour.

VERTEUIL: But how wonderful of you. I never thought you'd do it.

VALMONT: It seemed pointless to delay.

MERTEUIL: With anticipated results?

VALMONT: She was prostrate when I left. I called back the

63

following day.

MERTEUIL: You went back?

VALMONT: Yes, but she declined to receive me.

MERTEUIL: You don't say.

VALMONT: Subsequent enquiries I made established that she had withdrawn to a convent.

MERTEUIL: Indeed.

VALMONT: And she's still there. A very fitting conclusion, really. It's as if she'd been widowed. *(He reflects for a moment, then turns to MERTEUIL, radiating confidence.)* You kept telling me my reputation was in danger, but I think this may well turn out to be my most famous exploit. I believe it sets a new standard. I think I could confidently offer it as a challenge to any potential rival for my position. Only one thing could possibly bring me greater glory.

MERTEUIL: What's that?

VALMONT: To win her back.

MERTEUIL: You think you could?

VALMONT: I don't see why not.

MERTEUIL: I'll tell you why not: because when one woman strikes at the heart of another, she seldom misses; and the wound is invariably fatal.

VALMONT: Is that so?

MERTEUIL: I'm so convinced it's so, I'm prepared to offer any odds you care to suggest against your success. *(Some of the self-satisfaction has ebbed out of VALMONT's expression.)* You see, I'm also inclined to see this as one of my greatest triumphs.

VALMONT: There's nothing a woman enjoys as much as a victory over another woman.

MERTEUIL: Except, you see, Vicomte, my victory wasn't over her.

VALMONT: Of course it was, what do you mean?

MERTEUIL: It was over you. *(Long silence. The fear returns to VALMONT's eyes. He begins to look concerned. MERTEUIL, on the other hand, has never seemed more serene.)* That's what's so amusing. That's what's so genuinely delicious.

VALMONT: You don't know what you're talking about.

LES LIAISONS DANGEREUSES

MERTEUIL: You loved that woman, Vicomte. What's more you still do. Quite desperately. If you hadn't been so ashamed of it, how could you possibly have treated her so viciously? You couldn't bear even the vague possibility of being laughed at. And this has proved something I've always suspected. That vanity and happiness are incompatible. *(VALMONT is very shaken. He's forced to make a great effort, before he can resume, his voice a touch ragged with strain.)*

VALMONT: Whatever may or may not be the truth of these philosophical speculations, the fact is it's now your turn to make a sacrifice.

MERTEUIL: Is that right?

VALMONT: Danceny must go.

MERTEUIL: Where?

VALMONT: I've been more than patient about this little whim of yours, but enough is enough and I really must insist you call a halt to it. *(Silence.)*

MERTEUIL: One of the reasons I never remarried, despite a quite bewildering range of offers, was the determination never again to be ordered around. I decided if I felt like telling a lie, I'd rather do it for fun than because I had no alternative. So I must ask you to adopt a less marital tone of voice.

VALMONT: She's ill, you know. I've made her ill. For your sake. So the least you can do is get rid of that colourless youth.

MERTEUIL: I should have thought you'd have had enough of bullying women for the time being. *(VALMONT's face hardens.)*

VALMONT: Right. I see I shall have to make myself very plain. I've come to spend the night. I shall not take at all kindly to being turned away. *(MERTEUIL briefly consults the clock on her desk.)*

MERTEUIL: I am sorry. I'm afraid I've made other arrangements. *(A grim satisfaction begins to enliven VALMONT's features.)*

VALMONT: Ah. I knew there was something. Something I had to tell you. What with one thing and another, it had slipped my mind.

MERTEUIL: What?

VALMONT: Danceny isn't coming. Not tonight.

MERTEUIL: What do you mean? How do you know?

LES LIAISONS DANGEREUSES

VALMONT: I know because I've arranged for him to spend the night with Cécile. *(He smiles charmingly at MERTEUIL.)* Now I come to think of it, he did mention he was expected here. But when I put it to him that he really would have to make a choice, I must say he didn't hesitate for a second. I'd dictated a letter for Cécile to send him, as insurance, but as it turned out, there wasn't any need to be so cautious. He knew his mind.

MERTEUIL: And now I know yours.

VALMONT: He's coming to see you tomorrow to explain and to offer you, do I have this right, yes, I think so, his eternal friendship. As you said, he's completely devoted to you.

MERTEUIL: That's enough, Vicomte.

VALMONT: You're absolutely right. Shall we go up?

MERTEUIL: Shall we what?

VALMONT: Go up. Unless you prefer, this, if memory serves, rather purgatorial sofa.

MERTEUIL: I believe it's time you were going. *(Silence.)*

VALMONT: No. I don't think so. We made an arrangement. I really don't think I can allow myself to be taken advantage of a moment longer.

MERTEUIL: Remember I'm better at this than you are.

VALMONT: Perhaps. But it's always the best swimmers who drown. Now. Yes or no? Up to you, of course. I wouldn't dream of trying to influence you. I therefore confine myself to remarking that a no will be regarded as a declaration of war. So. One single word is all that's required.

MERTEUIL: All right. *(She looks at VALMONT evenly for a moment, almost long enough for him to conclude that she has made her answer. But she hasn't. It follows now, calm and authoritative.)* War.

A MADHOUSE IN GOA
by Martin Sherman
Seaside resort, Corfu - 1966 - David (20's) - Mrs. Honey (60's)

David - A young American
Mrs. Honey - An outspoken widow

David is a repressed young American who encounters the gregarious Mrs. Honey while visiting Greece. One evening, the two share a bottle of wine and exchange their very different views on life.

(The veranda. Evening. DAVID is sitting at the table, writing in his journal. MRS. HONEY enters, wearing a nightgown. She is carrying a bottle of wine and two small glasses.)
MRS. HONEY: Sweet Jesus! What an evening. Do you hear a cow out there? I have some wine. And glasses. I couldn't sleep. I saw you on the veranda. I had waking dreams, do you know them? Amazing landscapes, but one eye is open. Cows are much too noisy. Nikos Kistos has invaded my dreams. Manically chopping my table up with an axe. Here. *(She sits at her table.)* Move over here, to the table in question. *(DAVID joins her at her table.)* They've waxed it. See? Have some retsina. It tastes like nail polish. I don't drink too often. But this evening...well...it just isn't right, some evenings aren't out there—in the world—not right... *(She pours him a glass of wine.)*
DAVID: *(takes the glass)* Thank you.
MRS. HONEY: Drink it down very fast. Nikos Kistos is an evil man, mind my words, he's planning something. I smell enemies. I do, I do. Mind my words.
DAVID: *(drinks his wine)* Oh, my God.
MRS. HONEY: A bit like lava, isn't it? Have another. *(She pours him another glass.)* Glory be, child, don't you want to unbutton something?
DAVID: *(drinks the wine)* Ohh!
MRS. HONEY: *(drinks her wine)* It's good for you. Go on. Another.
DAVID: I can't.

A MADHOUSE IN GOA

MRS HONEY: I insist.

DAVID: Well... *(She pours him another glass.)* O.K. *(giggles)* It tastes awful. *(drinks the wine)* Do you, do you, do you...?

MRS HONEY: What?

DAVID: Do you...? *(He pauses for breath.)*

MRS. HONEY: Speak up child.

DAVID: Do you know where the Levant is?

MRS. HONEY: Oh. Somewhere, dear. Definitely somewhere. Somewhere out there. *(drinks her wine)* We're not savouring this, are we? *(She pours DAVID another glass.)* Something to do with the Mediterranean. Places like Cyprus...Syria...Lebanon...

DAVID: *(drinks his wine)* Jesus!

MRS. HONEY: Do you know Beirut? That's probably part of the Levant. You must go there someday. It's an absolute jewel. I travel, you know—place to place to place... *(She pours herself another glass.)* My, this stuff grows on you. I'm never anywhere for too long. They know my name at every American Express office in Europe and Asia. Not Australia. Doesn't interest me. I have this table reserved for another ten days. Damn Nikos Kistos! I don't want to move. *(drinks the wine)* A tiny bit more? *(She pours another glass.)* Well. Beirut. Now, I'm not partial to nightclubs but in Beirut nightclubs are as natural as the sea. There's one that is, in fact, by the sea; it has a spectacular if rather grotesque stage show and, for a finale, a long, giant, life-size train winds its way across the nightclub floor, weaving around the tables, with chorus girls standing on top of the railway cars, and cages coming down from the ceiling, those too with chorus girls, and flowers raining down on the tables, and gold coins as well, falling past the chorus girls in the cages onto the chorus girls on the train. *(DAVID looks at her, dumbfounded.)* Lordy! What a silly thing to remember. Well. Beirut. *(She holds her glass up in a toast.)*

DAVID: *(holds his glass up)* Beirut.

MRS. HONEY: The glass is empty. I do get fond of certain places. Usually much later. After I've left. I'll give you the address of a lovely hotel there. And that nightclub. You will go there some day. On your travels. Nikos Kistos worries me, boy.

A MADHOUSE IN GOA

DAVID: I'm sick of my travels.

MRS. HONEY: He wants this table, he does. It's only a piece of wood. Such a fuss.

DAVID: I'm sick of my travels.

MRS. HONEY: And he's devious. And it's a King. Spells trouble.

DAVID: I'm sick of my travels.

MRS. HONEY: What? Oh. Which travels?

DAVID: These. Here. There. This summer. My summer in Europe. *(Pause.)*

MRS. HONEY: Where have you been?

DAVID: Everywhere.

MRS. HONEY: For instance?

DAVID: Paris.

MRS. HONEY: *(smiles)* Ah!

DAVID: It was horrible.

MRS. HONEY: Oh.

DAVID: London.

MRS. HONEY: Ummm.

DAVID: A nightmare.

MRS. HONEY: I see.

DAVID: Rome.

MRS. HONEY: Roma!

DAVID: I hated it.

MRS. HONEY: Hated it?

DAVID: Venice.

MRS. HONEY: Miserable?

DAVID: Miserable.

MRS. HONEY: *(laughs)* I think you need these last few drops... *(She empties the dregs of the wine bottle into his glass.)*

DAVID: Why is it so funny?

MRS. HONEY: Did you not find Venice a little, a bit, a tiny bit—itsy-bitsy bit—beautiful? *(She laughs again.)*

DAVID: Yes.

MRS. HONEY: Then why was it miserable?

DAVID: I don't know. Yes, I do. You see, it was me. I was...

A MADHOUSE IN GOA

MRS. HONEY: What?

DAVID: Nothing.

MRS. HONEY: Go on.

DAVID: No.

MRS. HONEY: Spit it out. *(laughs)* I used to say that to the dentist, spit it out. Of course, he said the same thing to his patients. I wonder who picked it up from whom. *(Pause.)*

DAVID: I was lonely.

MRS. HONEY: *(laughs)* Oh. I'm sorry. I have a laughing fit. I don't mean it. Glory be! Lonely? Dear, dear.

DAVID: No one has talked to me. You're the first person on this entire trip who has talked to me.

MRS. HONEY: It's all those buttons. You're so covered up. You do not invite conversation. I'm amazed you're not wearing a necktie. Are your parents the very religious type? Do they abhor the human body? I have heard that Orthodox Jews make love through a hole in the sheet—is that true of your parents?—and if so, do they tear a hole or is it meticulously cut? Well, well, well—you are not a happy specimen, are you? Still in school?

DAVID: Just out. Out. Into the darkness... *(He stands up—can't handle it—sits down again.)*

MRS. HONEY: And child, your hair. It's so homeless. Did you notice, in London, during your nightmare stay there, that some of the young men are now wearing their hair long and wild and quite beautiful? Let your hair grow, boy. And muss it a bit. And treat yourself to sideburns. And slash away your trousers. Yes—show us your legs. Do you have a shape to you? Let's see it, child.

DAVID: I'm drowning.

MRS. HONEY: Oh dear.

DAVID: I'm tottering...

MRS. HONEY: You're drunk.

DAVID: On the edge...

MRS. HONEY: Very drunk.

DAVID: Of an abyss! *(MRS. HONEY stares at him and starts to laugh again.)*

A MADHOUSE IN GOA

MRS. HONEY: I'm sorry.

DAVID: I don't have nice legs. *(He starts to cry.)* I'm drunk. Michael! Do you have more wine? My legs are scrawny. My kneecaps stick out. He doesn't love me at all. He lied to me.

MRS. HONEY: Shh! You will wake the hotel up. Nikos Kistos will have us arrested for drinking. He's planning something, Nikos Kistos. The King could order a firing squad.

DAVID: I'm burning!

MRS. HONEY: It's the sun. It was extremely strong this afternoon.

DAVID: I'm on fire.

MRS. HONEY: Or then again, he could try to poison me.

DAVID: I'm lost in an inferno! *(MRS. HONEY looks up.)*

MRS. HONEY: *(sharply)* Inferno? Dear, dear. Retsina, you old dog. Now, let's pull ourselves together.

DAVID: I'm so unhappy. I want to die! I want to join a kibbutz!

MRS. HONEY: Well, at least you have a sense of priority.

DAVID: I'm twenty-three...

MRS. HONEY: *That* old!

DAVID: So much of me has been washed away...

MRS. HONEY: You tend to over-dramatize, did you know that? Is that why you take photographs? Are you attracted to the threatre? Do you have any friends?

DAVID: I'm falling...falling...

MRS. HONEY: Oh, I'm no good at this. Mothering.

DAVID: Into the abyss...

MRS. HONEY: Never suited me. Ask my children. They loathe me for good reason.

DAVID: The abyss...

MRS. HONEY: No, child. It's not an inferno. It's not even a brushfire. It's not an abyss. Do you know what an abyss is?

DAVID: What?

MRS. HONEY: Watching the dentist disappear before your eyes. Cancer. That's an abyss. Watching his flesh melt away from his face. Watching a truck drive through his body every night. That's an abyss. Now dry your eyes and go to bed. We mustn't wake the evil Kistos up.

71

A MADHOUSE IN GOA

The Kisti. Where is his brother? *(She stands up and looks at the sea.)* Not being loved is nothing. Easy. Fact of life. The dentist didn't love me, certainly not after the first year, but then, I never stopped jabbering, so who can blame him? And I didn't love the dentist, he was a fairly tedious man, although that is no reason to die such a cruel death. No, I married him to get away from my parents' home, and I did, God knows, I did. He took me to Utah, to the desert, the clean, quiet empty desert, which, believe it or not, I much preferred to Mississippi. And I liked his last name. To be called Honey in perpetuity. Who could resist? And when he finally met his humourless maker I found I had nothing to do. But stare at the desert. The dentist was a companion, you see. He rarely spoke, and when he did it was usually about bleeding gums, but still, he was there, sitting next to me, boring me, but not with malice, and we took comfort in being bored together. But left alone, I was useless. All I was trained to do in Mississippi was to read magazines and chatter. My children fled from my endless chatter. My daughter married a man every bit as dull as the dentist, isn't that always the way? And my son, who has some spunk and brains, moved as far away as he could. They were both petrified I'd visit them, so they suggested I take a trip. I packed a suitcase. It's been four years and I'll never return. They send me money every few months. To American Express. And now I chatter in different locations for a few weeks at a time. And move on. And that, too, is an abyss.

DAVID: I'm embarrassed, I didn't mean to...

MRS. HONEY: My son sent a letter with his last cheque. He's left his job. He's heading for San Francisco with his wife. He says the world is changing. There's a new kind of life. He says. He has *hope*. Well. Glory Hallelujah, bless his soul. *And*—his hair is very long. He sent a photograph. I think he looks quite stunning. He's not much older than you. *(She brushes DAVID's hair.)* Please. Let it grow. *(Pause.)* Well, well, well. Time to return Nikos Kistos to my dreams. Time to close my eyes and see him pulling at my table, like a demented puppy. Down, Nikos, down! *(She brushes her hand across his face.)* Breathe a little. Let some fresh air in. Throw away your camera.

72

Forget your hurt. Forget your family. Buy some shorts. Have adventures. But first—go to sleep. Sleep is good for growing hair. *(She kisses him. He stares at her.)*

DAVID: Mrs. Honey?

MRS. HONEY: What?

DAVID: Your nightgown—is on upside down.

MRS. HONEY: Well, so it is. Fancy that.

(She leaves.)

MAIDS OF HONOR
by Joan Casademont
Suburban Boston - Present - Annie (30's) - Harry (30-40)

Annie - A woman confronting a former love
Harry - Annie's former love

Three sisters; Monica, Izzy and Annie, have gathered at their family home for Monica's wedding to a stock broker of questionable morality.   During the malestrom of activity surrounding the wedding, quiet Annie is confronted by her former fiance, Harry, who is catering the affair.

ANNIE: Come in. Sit down. Something.

HARRY: You're not gonna run up the steps?

ANNIE: I'm gonna wait a few minutes before I do this time.

HARRY: Keep me guessing.

ANNIE: Not really. *(Pause. HARRY comes nearer, watchful.)*

HARRY: Has Monica gotten a chance to try the strawberry galettes yet?

ANNIE: *(With a laugh)* Come on, Harry.

HARRY: They might be funny to you, to me it's serious business if a client isn't happy. Has she tried them?

ANNIE: I'm sure they're fine.

HARRY: You mean she didn't rave about how good they were and fall over dead?

ANNIE: I'm sure she will when she gets a chance. *(Pause.)* You want some coffee, juice, alcohol?

HARRY: Coffee'd be nice.

ANNIE: O-kay. *(SHE gets cup, spoon, coffee, napkin during following)* Same as before?

HARRY: Same as before. *(HE sits. Pause.)* So how are you, Annie? All I really wanted to know was how you were.

ANNIE: Good. Very happy alone, really. Very, very—well not THAT happy but happy.

HARRY: The work's going well?

ANNIE: Uh-huh.

74

MAIDS OF HONOR

HARRY: *(Delighted)* I knew it, I always knew it would! I just happen to be following the art scene in Los Angeles, because, you know, I just opened one of my stores there, so I've seen your reviews, I've read about your—talking sculptures. I'd love to see them, they sound—well, they sound positively ridiculous and wonderful.

ANNIE: They are both.

HARRY: *(Teasing)* Modest.

ANNIE: Modesty doesn't pay.

HARRY: Neither does a grudge.

ANNIE: It's not a grudge, Harry, it's a total lack of trust.

HARRY: How can you be proven wrong if you won't give me another chance? *(Pause. ANNIE shrugs.)* Is there someone else?

ANNIE: I'm too old for someone else. Why keep trying at something you're lousy at.

HARRY: I guess not.

ANNIE: Right. *(Pause.)*

HARRY: Annie, I'll say it again. I'll say it a million times if it'll help. If I had anything to do with you going to the hospital, I'm sorry. I was young and stupid and I'm sorry.

ANNIE: Repetition is not the answer.

HARRY: What is? *(Pause.)*

ANNIE: I don't know how to forgive you. If I do I'm afraid the earth will suddenly open up and swallow me. I'll disappear.

HARRY: No, Annie. With or without me you'll never disappear again, I know just by looking at you.

ANNIE: Looks can be deceiving.

HARRY: Could you return one of my calls, answer one of my letters?

ANNIE: A more reasonable person would've taken silence as a message.

HARRY: Can you say you don't love me? Say it only if it's true and I'll go away. I'll leave you alone and—happy. *(Pause.)*

ANNIE: *(Moving away.)* Look, Harry. I can't think about this. You don't understand what's going on here today. Monica is—well, Monica is... Never mind!

HARRY: Monica's in trouble.

MAIDS OF HONOR

ANNIE: No!

HARRY: She's upset. Is it the food?

ANNIE: No!

HARRY: Just checking. Can I help?

ANNIE: Monica should probably not be doing what she's about to do.

HARRY: She should marry Roger.

ANNIE: No! I mean, yes, maybe, but that's not what I mean. How do you know?

HARRY: She probably loves him.

ANNIE: Oh, well, fine, love. Big deal, love! What a crock! That's not all it takes, you know. Fidelity to some is also desirable. I can't imagine why, of course, but it is. *(Pause.)*

HARRY: I personally plan on being faithful to my wife. Go on.

ANNIE: Well so she's—she's doing the wrong thing. I mean if in fact it is the wrong thing.

HARRY: Is Chuck an alcoholic?

ANNIE: No!

HARRY: Is he violent?

ANNIE: Never!

HARRY: Is he unfaithful?

ANNIE: Of course not!

HARRY: *(Seizing his opportunity)* You mean there's a worse crime under the sun than making one sad little slip of infidelity when your fiancee lied to you and told you that she herself had been unfaithful when in fact she hadn't, she just made you think she was to test you and you failed that test in a fit of panic?... Of course she set you up to fail her, but you forgave her for that because you knew she was scared, she was terrified of marrying a man like her father and rightly so. Now, you regret in the deepest fibers of your being that cowardly slip you made and you know you'll never do it again if she would only forgive you, if she would only give you another chance... You mean to tell me there's something more unforgiveable under the sun than having been terrified in your twenties of a lifelong commitment to a person who didn't believe it was possible? *(Pause.)*

ANNIE: I suppose there is, yes.

MAIDS OF HONOR

HARRY: God, I want a witness!

ANNIE: You just want to win! You've always had to win, Harry. Admit it.

HARRY: I care more now about two things. Food and you. Not in that order. If you refuse to have me now I still plan on taking over the world with my food.

ANNIE: Not so fast, I'm not gonna just resume!

HARRY: You're gonna deliberate for the next five years?

ANNIE: Let me think! Let me think now and deal with this wedding!... I do have to stop my sister from ruining her own chances, I do! *(Pause. ANNIE looks out screen door, upset.)* She's setting herself up to confirm that she's—unlovable, like he said.

HARRY: She's always listened to you. Tell her she's not.

ANNIE: *(Looking out)* Here come Izzy and Joel!

HARRY: Would you get her to try the strawberry galettes?

ANNIE: You'd better go.

HARRY: Go? Do I have to wait five years to call you?

ANNIE: Tomorrow.

HARRY: Tomorrow?

ANNIE: Tomorrow, Harry. That's it, take it or leave it! *(SHE opens the door for him to leave. Pause. THEY grin at each other, laugh.)* You have something against tomorrow?

HARRY: No. *(HE grabs her face, kisses her passionately and quickly.)* It's about time.

MY CHILDREN! MY AFRICA!
by Athol Fugard
Camdeboo, South Africa - 1985 - Thami (16-18) - Isabel (16-18)

Thami - A young man caught up in the struggle against apartheit
Isabel - Thami's white friend, fighting to understand the system
        that governs them both

Thami and Isabel are brought together at a school debate and
their ensuing friendship seems capable of transcending the
tragedy of apartheit until Thami's involvement in a violent
student boycott indirectly leads to the murder of their favorite
teacher, Mr. M. Here, Thami and Isabel say their good byes.

(THAMI waiting. ISABEL arrives.)
THAMI: Isabel.
ISABEL: *(It takes her a few seconds to respond.)* Hello, Thami.
THAMI: Thank you for coming.
ISABEL: *(SHE is tense. Talking to him is not easy.)* I wasn't going
to. Let me tell you straight out that there is nothing in this world...
nothing!...that I want to see less at this moment than anything or
anybody from the location. But you said in your note that it was
urgent, so here I am. If you've got something to say, I'll listen.
THAMI: Are you in a hurry?
ISABEL: I haven't got to be somewhere else, if that's what you mean.
But if you're asking because it looks as if I would like to run away
from here, from you!...very fast, then the answer is yes. But don't
worry, I'll be able to control that urge for as long as you need to say
what you want to.
THAMI: *(Awkward in the face of Isabel's severe and unyielding
attitude.)* I just wanted to say goodbye.
ISABEL: Again?
THAMI: What do you mean?
ISABEL: You've already done that, Thami. Maybe you didn't use that
word, but you turned your back on me and walked out of my life that
last afternoon the three of us... *(SHE can't finish.)* How long ago was
that?

78

MY CHILDREN! MY AFRICA!

THAMI: Three weeks I think.

ISABEL: So why do you want to do it again? Aren't you happy with the last time? It was so dramatic, Thami.

THAMI: *(Patiently.)* I wanted to see you because I'm leaving the town, I'm going away for good.

ISABEL: Oh, I see. This is meant to be a "sad" goodbye is it? *(SHE is on the edge.)* I'm sorry if I'm hurting your feelings but I thought you wanted to see me because you had something to say about recent events in our litttle community... *(Out of a pocket a crumpled little piece of newspaper which SHE opens with unsteady hands.)* ...a certain unrest related... I think that is the phrase they use...yes...here is is... *(Reading.)* "...unrest related incident in which according to witnesses the defenseless teacher was attacked by a group of blacks who struck him over the head with an iron rod before setting him on fire."

THAMI: Stop it, Isabel.

ISABEL: *(Fighting hard for self-control.)* Oh, Thami I wish I could! I've tried everything, but nothing helps. It just keeps going around and around inside my head. I've tried crying. I've tried praying! I've even tried confrontation. Ja, the day after it happened I tried to get into the location. I wanted to find the witnesses who reported it so accurately and ask them: ...why didn't you stop it! There was a police roadblock at the entrance and they wouldn't let me in. They thought I was crazy or something and "escorted" me back into the safekeeping of two now very frightened parents.

There is nothing wrong with me! All I need is someone to tell me why he was killed. What madness drove those people to kill a man who had devoted his whole life to helping them. He was such a good man, Thami! He was one of the most beautiful human beings I have ever known and his death is the ugliest thing I have ever known.

THAMI: *(Gives her a few seconds to calm down. Gently.)* He was an informer, Isabel. Somehow or the other somebody discovered that Mr. M was an informer.

ISABEL: You mean that list of pupils taking part in the boycott? You call that informing?

THAMI: No. It was worse than that. He went to the police and gave

79

them the names and addresses of our political action committee. All of them were arrested after his visit. They are now in detention.

ISABEL: Mr. M did that?

THAMI: Yes.

ISABEL: I don't believe it.

THAMI: It's true, Isabel.

ISABEL: No! What proof do you have?

THAMI: His own words. He told me so himself. I didn't believe it either when he was first accused, but the last time I saw him, he said it was true, that he had been to the police.

ISABEL: *(Stunned disbelief.)* Mr. M? A police spy? For how long?

THAMI: No. It wasn't like that. He wasn't paid or anything. He went to the police just that one time. He said he felt it was his duty.

ISABEL: What do you mean?

THAMI: Operation Qhumisa...the boycotts and strikes, the arson... you know he didn't agree with any of that. But he was also very confused about it all. I think he wished he had never done it.

ISABEL: So he went to the police just once.

THAMI: Yes.

ISABEL: As a matter of conscience.

THAMI: Yes.

ISABEL: That doesn't make him an "informer," Thami!

THAMI: Then what do you call somebody who gives information to the police?

ISABEL: No! You know what that word really means, the sort of person it suggests. Was Mr. M one of those? He was acting out of concern for his people...you said so yourself. He though he was doing the right thing! You don't murder a man for that!

THAMI: *(Near the end of his patience.)* Be careful, Isabel.

ISABEL: Of what?

THAMI: The words you use.

ISABEL: Oh? Which one don't you like? Murder? What do you want me to call it..."an unrest related incident?" If you are going to call him an informer, then I am going to call his death murder!

THAMI: It was an act of self-defense.

MY CHILDREN! MY AFRICA!

ISABEL: By who?

THAMI: The People.

ISABEL: *(Almost speechless with outrage.)* What? A mad mob attacks one unarmed defenseless man and you want me to call it...

THAMI: *(Abandoning all attempts at patience. HE speaks with the full authority of the anger inside him.)* Stop it, Isabel! You just keep quiet now and listen to me. You're always saying you want to understand us and what it means to be black...well if you do, listen to me carefully now. I don't call it murder, and I don't call the people who did it a mad mob and yes, I do expect you to see it as an act of self-defense... listen to me!...blind and stupid but still self-defense.

He betrayed us and our fight for freedom. Five men are in detention because of Mr. M's visit to the police station. There have been other arrests and there will be more. Why do you think I'm running away?

How were those people to know he wasn't a paid informer who had been doing it for a long time and would do it again? They were defending themselves against what they thought was a terrible danger to themselves. What Anela Myalatya did to them and their cause is what your laws define as treason when it is done to you and threatens the safety and security of your comfortable white world. Anybody accused of it is put on trial in your courts and if found guilty they get hanged. Many of my people have been found guilty and have been hanged. Those hangings *we* call murder!

Try to understand, Isabel. Try to imagine what it is like to be a black person, choking inside with rage and frustration, bitterness, and then to discover that one of your own kind is a traitor, has betrayed you to those responsible for the suffering and misery of your family, of your people. What would you do? Remember there is no magistrate or court you can drag him to and demand that he be tried for that crime. There is no justice for black people in this country other than what we make for ourselves. When you judge us for what happened in front of the school four days ago just remember that you carry a share of the responsibility for it. It is your laws that have made simple, decent black people so desperate that they turn into "mad mobs."

81

MY CHILDREN! MY AFRICA!

(ISABEL has been listening and watching intently. It looks as if SHE is going to say something but SHE stops herself.)
THAMI: Say it, Isabel.
ISABEL: No.
THAMI: This is your last chance. You once challenged me to be honest with you. I'm challenging you now.
ISABEL: *(SHE faces him.)* Where were you when it happened, Thami? *(Pause.)* And if you were, did you try to stop them?
THAMI: Isn't there a third question, Isabel? Was I one of the mob that killed him?
ISABEL: Yes. Forgive me, Thami...please forgive me! ...But there is that question as well. Only once! Believe me, only once...late at night when I couldn't sleep. I couldn't believe it was there in my head, but I heard the words... "Was Thami one of the ones who did it?"
THAMI: If the police catch me, that's the question they will ask.
ISABEL: I'm asking you because... *(An open, helpless gesture.)* ...I'm lost! I don't know what to think or feel anymore. Help me. Please. You're the only one who can. Nobody else seems to understand that I loved him. *(This final confrontation is steady and unflinching on both sides.)*
THAMI: Yes, I was there. Yes, I did try to stop it. *(THAMI gives Isabel the time to deal with his answer.)* I knew how angry the people were. I went to warn him. If he had listened to me he would still be alive, but he wouldn't. It was almost as if he wanted it to happen. I think he hated himself very much for what he had done, Isabel. He kept saying to me that it was all over. He was right. There was nothing left for him. That visit to the police station had finished everything. Nobody would have ever spoken to him again or let him teach their children.
ISABEL: Oh, Thami, it is all so wrong! So stupid! That's what I can't take...the terrible stupidity of it. We needed him. All of us.
THAMI: I know.
ISABEL: Then why is he dead?
THAMI: You must stop asking these questions, Isabel. You know the answers.

MY CHILDREN! MY AFRICA!

ISABEL: They don't make any sense, Thami.

THAMI: I know what you are feeling. *(Pause.)* I also loved him. Doesn't help much to say it now, I know, but I did. Because he made me angry and impatient with his "oldfashioned" ideas, I didn't want to admit it. Even if I had, it wouldn't have stopped me from doing what I did, the boycott and everything, but I should have tried harder to make him understand why I was doing it. You were right to ask about that. Now...? *(A helpless gesture.)* You know the most terrible words in your language, Isabel? Too late.

ISABEL: Ja.

THAMI: I'll never forgive myself for not trying harder with him and letting him know...my true feelings for him. Right until the end I tried to deny it...to him, to myself.

ISABEL: I'm sorry I...

THAMI: That's all right.

ISABEL: Are the police really looking for you?

THAMI: Yes. Some of my friends have already been detained. They're pulling in anybody they can get their hands on.

ISABEL: Where are you going? Cape Town?

THAMI: No. That's the first place they'll look. I've written to my parents telling them about everything. I'm heading north.

ISABEL: To where?

THAMI: Far, Isabel. I'm leaving the country.

ISABEL: Does that mean what I think it does?

THAMI: *(Nods.)* I'm going to join the movement. I want to be a fighter. I've been thinking about it for a long time. Now I know it's the right thing to do. I don't want to end up being one of the mob that killed Mr. M—but that will happen to me if I stay here.

ISABEL: Oh, Thami.

THAMI: I know I'm doing the right thing. Believe me.

ISABEL: I'll try.

THAMI: And you?

ISABEL: I don't know what to do with myself, Thami. All I know is that I'm frightened of losing him. He's only been dead four days and I think I'm already starting to forget what he looked like. But the worst thing is that there's nowhere for me to go and...you know...just be near him. That's so awful. I got my father to phone the police but they said there wasn't enough left of him to justify a grave. What there was had been disposed of in a "Christian manner." So where do I go? The burnt-out ruins of the school? I couldn't face that.

THAMI: Get your father or somebody to drive you to the top of the Wapadsberg Pass. It's on the road to Craddock.

ISABEL: I know it.

THAMI: It was a very special place to him. He told me that it was there where it all started, where he knew what he wanted to do with his life...being a teacher, being the Mr. M we knew. You'll be near him up there. I must go now.

ISABEL: Do you need any money?

THAMI: No. Sala Kakuhle, Isabel. That's the Xhosa goodbye.

ISABEL: I know it. Asispumla taught me how to say it. Hamba Kakhule, Thami.

(THAMI leaves.)

THE PINK STUDIO
by Jane Anderson
France - Early 1900's - Henri (40-50) - Claudine (40's)

Henri Matisse - A famous artist
Claudine - Henri's strong-willed wife

Henri and Claudine are on holiday when Henri spots an old friend from their balcony and invites him up.

(We hear the ocean and laughing offstage. Claudine, in only a slip, runs to the balcony and stands there relishing the air.)
CLAUDINE: Henri, come out here! Oh, it's just magnificent! *(Henri ENTERS in his shirt tails.)* Come out on the balcony and feel the sun! Oh, isn't this lovely. I wish we could stay here all year.
(Henri joins her.)
HENRI: You're a magnificent woman.
CLAUDINE: Thank you.
HENRI: I want to see you naked against the sea.
CLAUDINE: I know, Love. Oh, Henri, do you know what I'd like to do? I'd like to take you down to the flower market. Shall we do that?
HENRI: Yes, I'd like to see you naked there.
CLAUDINE: Stop. Oh, I have to take you there. You won't believe how many flowers there are. Carnations are in season. I love carnations. Let's buy bunches of them and bring them back to the room.
HENRI: *(bending over the balcony)* Hallo! Derain! Hallo! How the hell are you! *(back to Claudine)* Claudine, Derain is here.
CLAUDINE: *(not thrilled)* Oh, good.
HENRI: *(to Derain)* What? We just arrived last night. I'm here with Claudine! We just finished making love!
CLAUDINE: Henri, are you mad?!
HENRI: What a woman! I love her, Derain!
CLAUDINE: *(over this)* Henri! For God's sake!
HENRI: *(to Derain)* Yes come up! Come up! Room number Twenty.
CLAUDINE: Do you think anyone on the beach missed that?

THE PINK STUDIO

HENRI: *(to Claudine)* Derain looks marvelous. The sun suits him. He's as dark as a Turk.

CLAUDINE: What the hell is wrong with you?

HENRI: What?

CLAUDINE: Oh please. You know you were showing off for Derain.

HENRI: Not at all!

CLAUDINE: Why do you do things like that?

HENRI: Don't be mad at me, my Love.

CLAUDINE: Derain is coming up?

HENRI: Yes. I thought we all might go out to lunch.

CLAUDINE: I thought we were going to the flower market.

HENRI: He can come too.

CLAUDINE: This was something I wanted to do with you.

HENRI: I know, but Derain is a friend. He'd be crushed if we didn't see him.

CALUDINE: Let me make the bed.

HENRI: The chambermaid will do it.

CLAUDINE: Derain will see it.

HENRI: He doesn't care.

CLAUDINE: I do. *(Claudine grabs her dress and exits to where to bed is.)*

PLAYERS IN A GAME
by Dale Wasserman
Prague - 1316 - Anna (20's) - Richard (20's)

Anna - A beautiful zealot
Richard - A charming rascal

Anna is a self-righteous young woman who has complained to the Grand Inquisitor that immoralities abound in Prague and that they are perpetrated by a young rogue known as Richard the Healer. When Richard hears that he has been denounced to the Inquisition by Anna, he pays her a clandestine visit, and we see that her piety is not match for his powers of seduction.

RICHARD: *(Improvising a song)*
I sing the lay of a frozen lady,
Her thighs are snowy, her eyes are cold,
Her breast is a place of glaciers—
Oh, pray for a lover who's warm and who's bold.
    Weep, weep for the frozen lady,
    Maiden so virginal, maiden so cold,
    Pray, pray for the frozen lady,
    Pray for a lover who's warm and who's bold...
(He continues humming and strumming.)
ANNA: *(With the tension of a suppressed sexual-hysteric.)* He stands there. Watching my window. Waiting. For what? What does he want of me? *(Another tone.)* Or I of him? *(Sudden rage.)* I could have him whipped. Set my servants upon him, tell them, "Beat him till he bleeds! Seize him, strip him of his clothing, beat him with iron rods until he begs, until he cries out my name, until he pleads with me for..." *(Another change; haughtiness.)* No. Better say to him, "Take yourself to hell. There are other houses in Prague...houses where you wouldn't have to wait five minutes before they'd let you in. I could name those houses—and their mistresses. But this is the house of Anna Sarban. At *this* house—" *(She breaks, bending, suddenly in tears.)* God, you know I do not want this. *(She goes to the "window," opens it. Richard straightens up. They look at each other across the distance.*

87

PLAYERS IN A GAME

Richard crosses, enters her house. They confront each other face to face.) What do you want?

RICHARD: I am a healer.

ANNA: I have neither corns or cholera.

RICHARD: *(Studying her.)* They say if you can take three things from a woman all the rest of her is yours. *(He reaches out, very deliberately, to remove the diamond pendants from Anna's ears.)* One. Two. *(He reaches for the cross at the cleavage of her breasts. Anna steps back.)* Are you afraid of me?

ANNA: Not in the least.

RICHARD: Why are you trembling?

ANNA: Only my body.

RICHARD: I would not hurt you.

ANNA: You are hurting my honor.

RICHARD: Visits to the Inquisitor don't hurt your honor?

ANNA: I was there. What of it?

RICHARD: What did you tell him?

ANNA: I am not accountable to you! *(Richard waits.)* I told him of a certain house in St. Martin's Wall. You know that house, don't you? Of course—you've got a hand in every vice in Prague.

RICHARD: That house is used for prayer meetings.

ANNA: Oh, likely!

RICHARD: The lay brotherhood of Saint Lambert de Begny meets there.

ANNA: *(Mocking.)* Saint Lambert de Begny.

RICHARD: Why can't you believe I might be honest?

ANNA: Because you're a scoundrel! Capable of anything! You are the personification of all that is ungodly in Prague. Nothing more to life than a good time, eh? You and your Bishop—oh, *he's* an example, isn't he? With his young girls. As long as he was able he got every one of them in trouble!

RICHARD: Leave the Bishop out of it!

ANNA: Loyalty? To your master in sin?

RICHARD: I warn you!

ANNA: Threaten your whores if you like. Not Anna Sarban.

PLAYERS IN A GAME

RICHARD: What is it to you? My life is mine. What matter to you whether I give it to God or the Devil? You...are a rock of righteousness. How can my wickedness touch *you*? *(Anna turns her back on him.)* Very well, I'm a gambler. Not ashamed of it. The world of dice is...comprehensible. Six sides, nothing more. Rules anyone can understand. But this world of yours? You find out the rules only after you've played. Life is not an honest game!

ANNA: *(Scornfully.)* You ought to confess those feelings.

RICHARD: To whom—the Inquisitor?

ANNA: Have you finished?

RICHARD: Just a moment. I'm a scoundrel, right enough. But I play with my own money. My own life. Not with the lives of others. Not, for instance, with the life of my uncle.

ANNA: *(Puzzled.)* Your uncle?

RICHARD: *Your* uncle. Your uncle Ruthard is a member of our... religious group?

ANNA: You're lying!

RICHARD: You should ask. You might find other friends of yours. Friends you could wave goodbye to at the executioner's block. Do you know they cut off your right hand for playing dice? Hardly anyone survives it. I doubt your uncle Ruthard would, he's getting along in years. There's no blood in a dice game but there could be in yours.

ANNA: We must be responsible for our actions!

RICHARD: Oh, no, say it plain! You want me to be responsible for *your* actions.

ANNA: If you break the law you must be ready to pay.

RICHARD: But only when someone accuses! Well, here's an accuser. An elegant one. Never lost a penny at Martin's Wall. Doesn't even know who she's accusing. But still she accuses!

ANNA: Get out.

RICHARD: You didn't know anyone who goes to Martin's Wall. Only me. *I* am the one you want punished.

ANNA: Get out before I call for help!

RICHARD: Why, Anna? Could this be the reason? *(He kisses her. Anna stands very still. Her eyes close. Richard's hand caresses her throat, her breasts.)* If they cut off my hand I wouldn't be able to do *this...*

ANNA: *(Pitifully.)* Please...

RICHARD: Why did you go to the Inquisitor?

ANNA: Keep the earrings, you can sell them.

RICHARD: *(Caressing her.)* Say it, Anna. Call it by its name.

ANNA: It has not name.

RICHARD: Poor Anna. Locked up inside her own skin.

ANNA: *(Pulling away, violently.)* Don't patronize me!

RICHARD: I can teach you to be free. It's very enjoyable, Anna. It's not safe but it's enjoyable.

ANNA: How many women have you said that to already?

RICHARD: Hundreds. Send your servants away, I'll spend the night with you.

ANNA: And then? *(Richard reaches out, snaps the chain at her throat and holds the diamond cross in his hand.)*

RICHARD: Three.

RACING DEMON
by David Hare
London - Present - Frances (30) - Rev. Tony Ferris (20's)

Frances - An attractive ad executive
Rev. Tony Ferris - A passionate young vicar

Following an afternoon of lovemaking, Frances and Tony
discuss their relationship. The idealistic young Vicar has
already decided to end things but flounders when faced with
Frances's earnestness.

*(Frances's living room. A flat in South London. FRANCES PARNELL
is thirty, blonde. She is lying on the floor, covered by a sheet. The
REVEREND TONY FERRIS is younger than she is, sitting on a hard
chair at the end of the sheet. He has a loose-fitting modern suit, and
a dog collar. He has wavy black hair and a fresh, open face.)*
FRANCES: What happened then?
TONY: Oh, you know. Have I never told you?
FRANCES: No.
(They both smile.)
TONY: I was just a boy from the provinces. This was my first trip to
London. I was only sixteen. I was incredibly lonely. I was thinking,
all right, I'm frightened, I'm on my own, what would help would be if
I could buy a small crucifix. This was in Oxford Street. There was a
gift shop. I talked to the girl behind the counter. 'I think I've seen
one,' she said. She seemed a bit puzzled. So she went into the back.
Then when she came out, she had a couple. She said, 'Oh, I don't
think you'll want this one. It's got a little man on it.'
FRANCES: Yes. *(They laugh.)* That's funny.
TONY: I mean, where had she been all her life?
FRANCES: I don't know, though. I worked in a shop. Before I
started in advertising. It was just like that.
(TONY looks down at her a moment.)
TONY: Are you going to get dressed?
FRANCES: *(Smiles.)* If you like. Does it make you uncomfortable?
TONY: No.
FRANCES: You always dress first.

91

RACING DEMON

TONY: Lot to do.

FRANCES: Do you have time for a pizza?

TONY: If you hurry.

(She gets up, gathering the sheet around her. She goes out to change. TONY is thoughtful, not moving from his chair. He calls through to the bedroom.)

TONY: It's just tonight I want to work on a scheme I have. Which I want to put to the team. I've got an idea for common worship, to try and involve the Catholics and Methodists as well. I wanted to start with a day for World Peace. Or something. If we could get everyone together it would be the most incredible coup. It would really...

(FRANCES has come back in. She has pulled on jeans and a shirt. TONY stops speaking when she re-appears, as if censoring himself.)

FRANCES: What?

TONY: No then I think we'd really get people talking. Christ would be bang in the centre of things.

(FRANCES moves across the room and gets a hair-brush. She starts brushing her hair. TONY, still in his chair, looks down.)

TONY: I'm sorry.

FRANCES: No.

TONY: I can tell what you're thinking.

FRANCES: It's always Christ. We're alone. We make love. We have a little time. *(Smiles.)* And then Christ enters the room.

TONY: Yes. Well he's there. He's always with us.

FRANCES: I always pretend you're no different from anyone else. But you are. You always bring your friend to the party.

TONY: I can't help it.

FRANCES: I know. *(They both smile. She crosses the room to put her coat on, easily running her hand across his back as she goes.)* And is he coming for a pizza?

TONY: Inevitably.

FRANCES: And will he stay the night?

TONY: He will. But I can't.

FRANCES: Oh really?

TONY: No. Didn't I mention my aunt's coming down?

(She looks at him a moment.)

92

FRANCES: No. You forgot.
TONY: Yes. Aunt Ethel. She's ridiculously proud of me. I think she'd have preferred a nice smart parish in Surrey. But I explained I had to have the challenge of somewhere really difficult.
FRANCES: And when's she coming?
TONY: Oh, you know. This evening.
FRANCES: Mmm.
(She stands a moment, her coat on. She's ready to go. TONY doesn't get up.)
TONY: It's getting rather late for my meeting. I think I'll skip the pizza. Do you mind?
FRANCES: How long have you been here? Forty-five minutes?
TONY: Yes. I'm sorry. *(Looks down again.)* It's very wrong.
(She looks at him a moment, then starts to move away.)
FRANCES: Well, certainly it doesn't make me feel very valued...
TONY: I know. *(Tries to rally.)* This ecumenical thing could be very important. I do need a way to make my mark.
FRANCES: I understand that.
TONY: I don't mean for myself. It would be a contribution to the whole life of the Church.
FRANCES: Well, I'm sure. That's fine. As long as you're honest.
TONY: Why, yes.
FRANCES: Is Aunt Ethel really coming?
TONY: Why do you say that?
FRANCES: Because I can tell when you're lying.
(TONY is very subdued.)
TONY: Yes. Tomorrow she is. *(FRANCES is very still.)* Look, I'm sorry...
FRANCES: It's all right. I don't want an explanation.
TONY: No, really.
FRANCES: I'd rather not. It'll be humiliating. For both of us.
TONY: I'm going to feel rotten. In fact I do feel rotten already. Unless you let me share what I think. *(He waits, but she says nothing.)* I mean, I know this sounds terrible, but the fact is, our relationship... well, *we* understand. It's a caring and loving relationship, with some eventual purpose. It's in the context of...well, of our future. Of one

day marrying. I mean we've sort of joked about it. But I think that's what we've both thought. Haven't we? *(He pauses. She doesn't answer.)* I mean, you know I would *never*...the physical experience, I mean, you understand it's always in the context of a long-term commitment. An idea, if you like. Which both of us have. And which is terrible exciting.

FRANCES: But?

(He looks at her mistrustfully.)

TONY: But I have been getting worried how it may look to the rest of the world. *(He gets up quickly to stifle her reaction.)* I mean, you know I don't have any hang-ups. Personally. The biblical evidence is pretty inconclusive. We all know. We have advanced. Paul wasn't Jesus. You can read the Bible either way. All that so-called Christian morality, we understand it can be too narrowly interpreted. It's a question of what feels right in your heart. And with you it's always felt right. I promise you. I believe in the expression of God's love through another human being. In a serious context, it's good. But lately I don't know...it's made me uneasy.

FRANCES: Uneasy in yourself?

TONY: Yes. Partly.

FRANCES: Or uneasy for what the Bishop might say?

TONY: *(Indignant)* You know that's not fair.

FRANCES: Isn't it? I can see you're frightened. I'm not sure why. Either it's your conscience or else you just don't want to get caught.

TONY: Please.

FRANCES: Well, which is it?

TONY: It isn't that easy.

FRANCES: Isn't it?

TONY: No.

(Now she is very quiet, fearful.)

FRANCES: Do you confess me?

TONY: No. No, of course not. But I don't really believe in confession. *(He looks miserably across at her, aware of how feeble this sounds.)* I wonder sometimes if a non-believer can get hold of these problems at all.

(FRANCES walks across the room and gets his raincoat.)

RACING DEMON

FRANCES: You'd better go. You'll be late for your meeting.

TONY: I can't go.

FRANCES: Why not?

TONY: Don't be ridiculous. I've told you my side. I've tried to communicate my thoughts.

FRANCES: Well, you have.

TONY: But what do you think?

FRANCES: Nothing. *(Shakes her head.)* Honestly, I have nothing to say.

(TONY stands. He is gentle now.)

TONY: Frances. Please say.

FRANCES: What does it matter? You've come this far without talking to me. It had to be dragged from you as it was. I feel I'm no longer even part of this. You've started not to look at me. Aren't I irrelevant? Aren't you in an argument with God? *(Hands across his coat.)* Here's your coat. *(Stops, close to him now.)* And look—for the record—I didn't make love in any 'context'. Whatever that may mean. I made love because I wanted you. Is that really such a terrible idea? *(He smiles, a warmth suddenly reappearing between them.)* I liked your innocence. You came up from Bristol, you were a Christian. All right, I got over that. Because your faith was fresh. It was simple. You managed to be a normal person as well. Yes, well exactly. It's a high compliment. After my childhood. *(Turns away.)* But it's over.

TONY: No, Frances. I'm not saying that.

FRANCES: No, I am. You've got the bug. I've seen it before. *(Shakes her head, quiet now.)* All you want is to carry the Cross.

TONY: Not at all. Look, it's just...it's terribly complicated. It's team ministry. There are three churches. We try to minister to the whole area's needs. It is very exciting. It's also demanding. So anything that... *(He pauses, disastrously.)*

FRANCES: That what?

TONY: I don't know how to put this...anything that dissipates my energy...

(FRANCES is suddenly furious.)

FRANCES: Yes, well, I think you should definitely leave.

(But TONY rides on top of her, confronting her at last.)

95

RACING DEMON

TONY: It was exciting. It was wonderful. You know. All through ordination. No question, it was you who got me through. After everything. In every way, it was such a tough time. 'Am I worthy? Am I really up to it? Fulfilling God's mission on earth?' I found being with you in the evening was restful. It seemed natural. Just to walk on the common. Listen to your office gossip. Not thinking about theology. But it's got harder since then. *(Looks at her anxiously.)* I've got frightened of drift. I want to be purposeful. I don't want complication in this new life. There must be 10 million people in this city, not a tenth of them have any idea what it is to experience God's love. Oh, it sounds stupid, I can see you laughing...

FRANCES: I'm not.

TONY: Look where we're working. It's nowhere, it isn't Brixton, it isn't even Kennington. Basically it's just a horrid great road surrounded by council estates. With thousands of people whose lives could be infinitely richer. It's my job to give them some sense of joy. How can I get on with it unless...unless my own private life is sort of cleared out the way? *(She just looks at him.)* At the moment it's messy. When I wake up, I think, today's the day I shall see her. Of course I'm thrilled. But also I feel a kind of dread. It raises questions. It's a feeling in my stomach. *(Shakes his head.)* I'm not sure I can afford that any more.

(FRANCES is very quiet.)

FRANCES: No, well, plainly.

TONY: You've been so good for me. You know I'll always want to be friends.

FRANCES: Why is there one word you're frightened to use?

TONY: Which one? *(Frowns.)* What word?

FRANCES: I'm not a Christian, so it doesn't frighten me.

TONY: I have no idea what you mean.

FRANCES: *(Smiles)* The word is sin. Why don't you use it? You've been sinning.

(He looks at her, silenced.)

FRANCES: Well, isn't that what you think?

TEMPTATION
by Vaclav Havel
translated by Marie Winn
Vilma's apartment - Present - Foustka (30-40) - Vilma (30's)

Foustka - A scientist tempted by a mysterious stranger to dabble
        in witchcraft
Vilma - Foustka's lover

Vilma and Foustka are both scientists working at an institute in
undisclosed research. Feeling a need for a change, the two
lovers decide that their relationship needs a bit of spicing up.
To accomplish this end they act out a scene which involves a
dancer, some violets and jealousy.

*(Vilma's apartment. It is a cozy boudoir, furnished with antiques.
There is a door at the rear. At the left is a large bed with a canopy.
At the right are two small armchairs, a large Venetian mirror, and a
vanity table with a large collection of perfumes on it. Scattered about
the room are various female odds and ends and trinkets. The only thing
folded neatly is Foustka's evening outfit next to the bed. The colors are
all feminine, predominantly pink and purple. As the curtain rises,
Foustka is sitting in his undershorts at the edge of the bed, and Vilma,
in a lacy slip, is sitting at the vanity table combing her hair, facing the
mirror with her back to Foustka. A short pause.)*

FOUSTKA: When was he here last?

VILMA: Who?

FOUSTKA: Stop asking stupid questions!

VILMA: You mean that dancer? About a week ago.

FOUSTKA: Did you let him in?

VILMA: He just brought me some violets. I told him I had no time,
that I was hurrying to meet you.

FOUSTKA: I asked you whether you let him in.

VILMA: I don't remember anymore...maybe he came in for a
moment.

FOUSTKA: So you kissed him!

VILMA: I kissed him on the cheek to thank him for the violets, that's

97

all.

FOUSTKA: Vilma, don't treat me like a fool, for goodness sake! I just bet you could buy him off with a mere kiss on the cheek once you let him in! Surely he tried to dance with you at the very least.

VILMA: Henry, drop it, for goodness sake! Can't you talk about anything more interesting?

FOUSTKA: Did he try or not?

VILMA: All right, he did, if you really must know! But I won't tell you another thing! I simply refuse to keep talking to you on this level, because it's embarrassing, undignified, insulting, and ridiculous! You know very well that I love you, and that no dancer could possibly be a threat to you, so stop tormenting yourself with this endless cross-examination! I don't keep pumping you for details either—and I'd have far more reason to do so!

FOUSTKA: So you refuse to tell? Well in that case eveything is quite clear.

VILMA: But I've told you a hundred times that I don't go out of my way to see him, I don't care for him, I don't dance with him, so what else am I supposed to do, damn it!

FOUSTKA: He hangs around you, he flatters you, he wants to dance with you all the time—and you enjoy it! If you didn't enjoy it, you'd have gotten rid of him long ago.

VILMA: I won't deny that I enjoy it—any woman would enjoy it. His persistence is touching, and so is the very fact that he never gives up, even though he knows perfectly well that he doesn't have a chance. Would you, for instance, be capable of driving here at night from God knows where for no other reason than to bring me some violets, even though you knew the situation was hopeless?

FOUSTKA: He's persistent because you deliberately dash his hopes in a way that keeps them alive and you deliberately reject him in a way that makes him long for you more and more! If you really slammed the door on his hopes he'd never show up here again. But you wouldn't do that, because it amuses you to play cat and mouse with him. You're a whore!

VILMA: You've decided to insult?

TEMPTATION

FOUSTKA: How long did you dance together?

VILMA: Enough, Henry, you're beginning to be disgusting! I've always known that you're eccentric, but I really never suspected that you're capable of being this nasty! What's suddenly brought on this pathological jealousy of yours? This insensitivity, tactlessness, maliciousness, vengefulness? At least if you had any objective reason for it...

FOUSTKA: So you're planning to keep whoring around?

VILMA: You have no right to talk to me like that! You kept pawing at that girl all evening, everybody's embarrassed, I wander around like an idiot—people feel sorry for me all over the place—and now you have the nerve to reproach me! Me! You do as you damn well please, I just have to suffer in silence, and finally you make a scene here on account of some crazy dancer! Do you see how absurd it is? Do you realize how terribly unfair it is? Do you have the faintest idea of how selfish and cruel you are?

FOUSTKA: In the first place, I was certainly not pawing anyone and I'd like you to please refrain from using words like that, especially when you're referring to pure creatures like Marketa. In the second place, we're not discussing me, but you, so kindly stop changing the subject. Sometimes I get a feeling that there's some monstrous plan hidden behind all this. First, you'll resurrect feelings within me that I'd assumed were dead long ago, and then once you've deprived me thus of my well-known objectivity, you'll begin to tighten a web of deceit around my heart, lightly at first, but then ever more painfully, an especially treacherous one because it is composed of a multitude of delicate threads of dancerly pseudoinnocence! But I won't let myself be tortured on this rack any longer! I'll do something either to myself—or to him—or to you—or to all of us!

(Vilma puts down her comb, begins to clap her hands, and walks towards Foustka with a smile. Foustka also begins to smile, stands up, and walks towards Vilma.)

VILMA: You keep getting better and better!

FOUSTKA: You weren't bad yourself.

(Foustka and Vilma gently embrace, kiss, and then slowly get into bed

together. They settle down together comfortably, lean back against the pillows, and cover their legs with a blanket. Foustka lights a cigarette for himself and for Vilma. Vilma finally ends a long pause by speaking.)

VILMA: Henry.

FOUSTKA: Hmm...

VILMA: Isn't it beginning to get on your nerves just a bit?

FOUSTKA: What?

VILMA: You know, that I keep making you play these games.

FOUSTKA: It did bother me for quite a long time.

VILMA: And now?

FOUSTKA: Now just the opposite—it's beginning to scare me.

VILMA: To scare you? Why?

FOUSTKA; I have a feeling that I'm beginning to get into it too much.

VILMA *(Exclaiming)*: Henry! Don't tell me you're really beginning to get jealous! Now that's fantastic! Never in my wildest dreams did I hope it would succeed like this! I had become resigned to the idea that you'd never feel any jealousy other than the make-believe kind.

FOUSTKA: I'm sorry, but I can't share your delight.

VILMA: I don't understand what you're afraid of!

FOUSTKA: My own self!

VILMA: Come on!

FOUSTKA: Don't underestimate it, Vilma. Something's happening to me. I suddenly feel capable of doing all sorts of things that have always been alien to me. It's as if something dark inside of me were suddenly beginning to flow out of its hiding place and into the open.

VILMA: What an alarmist you are! You're beginning to feel a little healthy jealousy and that throws into a complete panic! There's nothing wrong with you. Maybe you're just a little upset because your situation at the Institute came to a head this evening with that unfortunate incident with the director. That's obviously on your mind, and it's working away at your unconscious, looking for some way out, even though you won't admit it. That's why you're beginning to see bogeymen all over the place.

FOUSTKA: If only it were that simple. *(Pause.)*

TEMPTATION

VILMA: Do you think he'll destroy you?

FOUSTKA: He'll certainly try. The question is whether he has enough power to do it.

VILMA: But he's got all the power he wants—all the power there is, actually—at least as far as we're concerned.

FOUSTKA: There are other kinds of power besides the kind he dispenses.

(Vilma, horrified, jumps and kneels on the pillow opposite Foustka.)

VILMA: Do you mean that seriously?

FOUSTKA: Hmm...

VILMA: Now you're scaring me! Promise me you won't dabble in that sort of thing!

FOUSTKA: And what if I won't promise?

VILMA: The minute you mentioned that cripple I knew there'd be hell to pay! He's addled your brains! You'd actually go so far as to get involved with him?

FOUSTKA: Why not?

VILMA: This is horrible!

FOUSTKA: At least you see that I wasn't just kidding around before.

THE TRAVELLING SQUIRREL
by Robert Lord
Manhattan - Present - Bart (20's-30's) - Jane (20's-30's)

Bart - A struggling writer
Jane - Bart's wife and soap opera star

A comedy about Bart and Jane, who have been married for several years. He is still struggling as a writer, working as a typesetter to support himself. She is a successful soap opea actress. Here, Bart tells Jane about an episode with an agent who hated his book.

JANE: Why didn't you call? I've been going out of my mind. How did it go? Did he love you? Of course he loved you.

BART: He hated me.

JANE: What?

BART: You heard. He hated me. He hated my book. We made eye contact. He said I was full of shit.

JANE: You're joking? You're making this up?

BART: I'm not a masochist.

JANE: I don't get it.

BART: Neither did he. He kept calling it a novel. I said it was a prose poem. Did he listen? No. He said there wasn't enough sex. I said it wasn't about sex, it was about love. He looked at me as if I was retarded. I made a fool of myself, Jane. A complete fool.

JANE: You didn't.

BART: I did. I was there. I know. He spoke to me in words of one syllable. Who am I kidding? He's probably right.

JANE: I loved it.

BART: It's probably dreadful. What did I think I was doing? What a jerk! Bart Babbington finishes a book and the world should pay attention?

JANE: Yes.

BART: Why? I wrote a turgid prose poem.

JANE: He said it was turgid?

BART: Turgid and short.

THE TRAVELLING SQUIRREL

JANE: This is all my fault.

BART: How? You didn't write it.

JANE: I shouldn't have introduced you to Terry. It was a big mistake. My instincts are usually excellent. I'm sorry. I thought it was the right thing to do. I was so excited about the book. After five years!

BART: You're making me feel worse. Five years! What a waste of time. I should've gone into the family business.

JANE: The United States Post Office is hardly a family business.

BART: Thanks.

JANE: I'm sorry. I want you to be a success. I want people to know how brilliant you are.

BART: I'm not brilliant.

JANE: You are. Oh, Bart...

BART: Bert! He couldn't even remember my name.

JANE: You poor darling.

BART: He remembered your name all right. He thinks you're "hot."

JANE: Who cares?

BART: Terry does. He thinks you're headed for major stardom. What am I going to do, Jane? You are hot. Everyone loves you. Everyone knows who you are. And I'm out in the cold.

JANE: No, you're not.

BART: I am. I'm no one. Nothing. Why did I ever finish it? If I hadn't finished the damn thing I might still believe in it.

JANE: It is good.

BART: You're only saying that because you love me.

JANE: Bart...?

BART: I think I need to be alone.

ZORA NEALE HURSTON
by Laurence Holder
Zora's imagination - Zora Neale Hurston - Langston Hughes

Zora Neale Hurston - A Visionary black American writer
Langston Hughes - Zora's partner and collaborator

Zora Neale Hurston was an outspoken and ground-breaking writer/anthropologist who devoted her creative talents to portraying American Blacks in an accurate and non-patronizing manner. This zeal produced such classics as "Mule Bone." For a time, she collaborated with Langston Hughes. Here, Hughes breaks up the partnership, citing philosophical and creative differences.

(Enter Langston)
ZORA: Oh, I had run down a patron, a woman. You see in those days, all us good ones could get someone to pay our way while they waited for us to get famous and make a lot of money. My patron was Mrs. Rufus Osgood Mason III. She insisted on being called Godmother.

> "By the warmth of my Godmother's love I am made to stand erect
>
> You are the Spring and Summer of my existence..."

Godmother darling, I really need a pair of shoes. You remember we discussed the matter in the fall and agreed that I should own only one pair at a time. I bought a pair in mid-December and they have held up until now. My big toe is about to burst out of my right shoe and so I must do something about it.

She wanted every conceivable kind of control on you. I mean everything. Sometimes if I want to go to the movies, I have to kiss ass.
LANGSTON: Well, that's the whole problem with this patron stuff. They control the way you walk, talk and look.
ZORA: "Zora, I want all of your material sent directly to me at my home on Park Avenue. You are so loose sometimes, I get the feeling that you aren't ready for the big time yet, and I don't want you to misuse your material."

ZORA NEALE HURSTON

LANGSTON: What does that mean, "misuse"?

ZORA: "Misuse"? It means I can't control my own material or work on anything else.

LANGSTON: You mean our work on MULE BONE has to be put aside.

ZORA: I didn't say that.

LANGSTON: Why did we hook with this thing? I mean, I was writing before I ever saw a patron.

ZORA: Because we need the money, Langston.

LANGSTON: You talked me into becoming a slave for this woman.

ZORA: It wasn't me, Langston. You saw the importance of having someone to take care of you so you could have the leisure time to think and write.

LANGSTON: I always had the leisure time before and I never had to account for myself or my time. But this Godmother is driving me crazy. And now we've got all this material and we can't do anything with it?

ZORA: We can do anything we want, we just have to wait. I want to work on MULE BONE too.

LANGSTON: Well, then, let's forget about Godmother.

ZORA: Langston, please, don't make it more difficult for me than it is. The woman pays the rent, buys the groceries. I get everything I want except shoes. "Shoes," she thinks, "are a luxury, child, you can ill afford. I suggest you put away those visions of grand shoes and concentrate on bringing to paper your observations of the growth and development of your people in this hemisphere."

LANGSTON: What am I supposed to do, huh? What am I supposed to do? Forget about me to take care of you?

ZORA: I took care of you. I sold your poetry when I was down South. The railroad workers loved it.

LANGSTON: Well, Zora, that money's gone.

ZORA: So what to do?

LANGSTON: I've given you a draft of the first two acts. You're supposed to be filling in the gaps with the folklore and the anthropology. You haven't done it yet. Why? Because of this mess with our patron. Well, where does that leave me, Zora? Out on a stick is where.

ZORA: Are you saying that I'm not doing my share?

LANGSTON: I'm saying more than that, my dear. I'm saying that you are holding me back because you are scared. You like working for those people. You work for the very people who you claim to despise, but you work for them. You put yourself in one of them mammy outfits you just love to wear with the headrags and the dumpled up cotton dresses and then you wear them down with your obsequiousness. You minstrel for them, Zora.

ZORA: I do what I have to do. I need the money.

LANGSTON: I can't trade my heart for cash. I'm going to do something with MULE BONE.

ZORA: What are you talking about? MULE BONE is just as much mine as it is yours.

LANGSTON: The name is mine. The first two acts are also, and I'll get some folklore from someplace else.

ZORA: Like hell you will! I've put in as many years as you have on it.

LANGSTON: You should get smart, you know. You really should. This travesty with our patron is a farce. She doesn't even like my work. Wants it to be authentic. As soon as I heard that word, I knew who was behind her thinking. You, Zora. You be up there on Park Avenue, reading my things behind my back, and she is up there listening to you. Zora, I write the way I want, and if Godmother doesn't want to read it or buy it, then it's all right with me. I'm not writing for the money. I'm writing for the privilege of being alive. It's something I have to do and if I didn't do it, then I'd die.

(EXIT LANGSTON)

SECTION II

Two Men

BETRAYAL
by Harold Pinter
Jerry's house - Spring, 1977 - Jerry (40's) - Robert (40's)

Jerry - A man having an affair
Robert - Jerry's lover's husband

Robert's wife has confessed her affair with his friend, Jerry. Here, the two men confront one another in Robert's study.

JERRY: It's good of you to come.
ROBERT: Not at all.
JERRY: Yes, yes, I know it was difficult... I know...the kids...
ROBERT: It's all right. It sounded urgent.
JERRY: Well... You found someone, did you?
ROBERT: What?
JERRY: For the kids.
ROBERT: Yes, yes. Honestly. Everything's in order. Anyway. Charlotte's not a baby.
JERRY: No. *(Pause.)* Are you going to sit down?
ROBERT: Well, I might, yes, in a minute. *(Pause.)*
JERRY: Judith's at the hospital...on night duty. The kids are...here...upstairs.
ROBERT: Uh-huh.
JERRY: I must speak to you. It's important.
ROBERT: Speak.
JERRY: Yes. *(Pause.)*
ROBERT: You look quite rough. *(Pause.)* What's the trouble? *(Pause.)* It's not about you and Emma, is it? *(Pause.)* I know all about that.
JERRY: Yes. So I've...been told.
ROBERT: Ah. *(Pause.)* Well, it's not very important, is it? Been over for years, hasn't it?
JERRY: It is important.
ROBERT: Really? Why? *(Jerry stands, walks about.)*
JERRY: I thought I was going to go mad.
ROBERT: When?

107

BETRAYAL

JERRY: This evening. Just now. Wondering whether to phone you. I had to phone you. It took me...two hours to phone you. And then you were with the kids... I thought I wasn't going to able to see you... I thought I'd go mad. I'm very grateful to you...for coming.

ROBERT: Oh for God's sake! Look, what exactly do you want to say? *(Pause. Jerry sits.)*

JERRY: I don't know why she told you. I don't know how she could tell you. I just don't understand. Listen, I know you've got...look, I saw her today...we had a drink...I haven't seen her for...she told me, you know, that you're in trouble, both of you...and so on. I know that. I mean I'm sorry.

ROBERT: Don't be sorry.

JERRY: Why not? *(Pause.)* The fact is I can't understand...why she thought it necessary...after all these years...to tell you...so suddenly...last night...

ROBERT: Last night?

JERRY: Without consulting me. Without even warning me. After all, you and me...

ROBERT: She didn't tell me last night.

JERRY: What do you mean? *(Pause.)* I know about last night. She told me about it. You were up all night, weren't you?

ROBERT: That's correct.

JERRY: And she told you...last night...about her and me. Did she not?

ROBERT: No, she didn't. She didn't tell me about you and her last night. She told me about you and her four years ago. *(Pause.)* So she didn't have to tell me again last night. Because I knew. And she knew I knew because she told me herself four years ago. *(Silence.)*

JERRY: What?

ROBERT: I think I will sit down. *(He sits.)* I thought you knew.

JERRY: Knew what?

ROBERT: That I knew. That I've known for years. I thought you knew that.

JERRY: You thought I knew?

ROBERT: She said you didn't. But I didn't believe that. *(Pause.)*

108

Anyway I think I thought you knew. But you say you didn't?

JERRY: She told you...when?

ROBERT: Well, I found out. That's what happened. I told her I'd found out and then she...confirmed...the facts.

JERRY: When?

ROBERT: Oh, a long time ago, Jerry. *(Pause.)*

JERRY: But we've seen each other...a great deal...over the last four years. We've had lunch.

ROBERT: Never played squash though.

JERRY: I was your best friend.

ROBERT: Well, yes, sure. *(Jerry stares at him and then holds his head in his hands.)* Oh, don't get upset. There's no point. *(Silence. Jerry sits up.)*

JERRY: Why didn't she tell me?

ROBERT: Well, I'm not her, old boy.

JERRY: Why didn't you tell me? *(Pause.)*

ROBERT: I thought you might know.

JERRY: But you didn't know for *certain*, did you? You didn't *know*!

ROBERT: No.

JERRY: Then why didn't you tell me? *(Pause.)*

ROBERT: Tell you what?

JERRY: That you knew. You bastard.

ROBERT: Oh, don't call me a bastard, Jerry. *(Pause.)*

JERRY: What are we going to do?

ROBERT: You and I are not going to do anything. My marriage is finished. I've just got to make proper arrangements, that's all. About the children. *(Pause.)*

JERRY: You hadn't thought of telling Judith?

ROBERT: Telling Judith what? Oh, about you and Emma. You mean she never knew? Are you quite sure? *(Pause.)* No, I hadn't thought of telling Judith, actually. You don't seem to understand. You don't seem to understand that I don't give a shit about any of this. It's true I've hit Emma once or twice. But that wasn't to defend a principle. I wasn't inspired to do it from any kind of moral standpoint. I just felt like giving her a good bashing. The old itch...you understand.

BETRAYAL

(Pause.)

JERRY: But you betrayed her for years, didn't you?

ROBERT: Oh yes.

JERRY: And she never knew about it. Did she?

ROBERT: Didn't she? *(Pause.)*

JERRY: I didn't.

ROBERT: No, you didn't know very much about anything, really, did you? *(Pause.)*

JERRY: No.

ROBERT: Yes you did.

JERRY: Yes I did. I lived with her.

ROBERT: Yes. In the afternoons.

JERRY: Sometimes very long ones. For seven years.

ROBERT: Yes, you certainly knew all there was to know about that. About the seven years of afternoons. I don't know anything about that. *(Pause.)* I hope she looked after you all right. *(Silence.)*

JERRY: We used to like each other.

ROBERT: We still do. *(Pause.)* I bumped into old Casey the other day. I believe he's having an affair with my wife. We haven't played squash for years, Casey and me. We used to have a damn good game.

JERRY: He's put on weight.

ROBERT: Yes, I thought that.

JERRY: He's over the hill.

ROBERT: Is he?

JERRY: Don't you think so?

ROBERT: In what respect?

JERRY: His work. His books.

ROBERT: Oh his books. His art. Yes his art does seem to be falling away, doesn't it?

JERRY: Still sells.

ROBERT: Oh, sells very well. Sells very well indeed. Very good for us. For you and me.

JERRY: Yes.

ROBERT: Someone was telling me—who was it—must have been someone in the publicity department—the other day—that when Casey

110

went up to York to sign his latest book, in a bookshop, you know, with Barbara Spring, you know, the populace queued for hours to get his signature on his book, while one old lady and a dog queued to get Barbara Spring's signature, on her book. I happen to think that Barbara Spring...is good, don't you?

JERRY: Yes. *(Pause.)*

ROBERT: Still, we both do very well out of Casey, don't we?

JERRY: Very well. *(Pause.)*

ROBERT: Have you read any good books lately?

JERRY: I've been reading Yeats.

ROBERT: Ah. Yeats. Yes. *(Pause.)*

JERRY: You read Yeats on Torcello once.

ROBERT: On Torcello?

JERRY: Don't you remember? Years ago. You went over to Torcello in the dawn, alone. And read Yeats.

ROBERT: So I did. I told you that, yes. *(Pause.)* Yes. *(Pause.)* Where are you going this summer, you and the family?

JERRY: The Lake District.

THE DRESSER
by Ronald Harwood

An English theatre - January, 1942 - Sir (60's) - Norman (50's)

Sir - An aging Shakesperian actor
Norman - Sir's dresser and longtime confidant

Sir is a man at the end of his life. Fighting illness and memory loss, he bravely prepares for his 227th performance of "King Lear." Norman, his loyal dresser, does his best to make sure that Sir gets to the stage looking and feeling his best.

SIR: Too many interruptions—my concentration—Norman!

NORMAN: Sir?

SIR: How does the play begin?

NORMAN: Which play, Sir?

SIR: Tonight's, tonight's, I can't remember my first line.

NORMAN: 'Attend the Lords of France and Burgundy, Gloucester.'

SIR: Yes, yes. What performance is this?

(NORMAN consults a small notebook)

NORMAN: Tonight will be your two hundred and twenty-seventh performance of the part, Sir.

SIR: Two hundred and twenty-seven Lears and I can't remember the first line.

NORMAN: We've forgotten something, if you don't mind my saying so.

(SIR looks at him blankly)

NORMAN: We have to sink our cheeks.

(SIR applies the appropriate make-up)

SIR: I shall look like this in my coffin.

NORMAN: And a broad straight line of Number Twenty down the nose. Gives strength, you say.

(SIR adds to the line down the nose and studies the result. NORMAN pours a little Brown and Polson's cornflour into a bowl)

SIR: Were you able to find any Brown and Polson's?

NORMAN: No, but I'm still looking. There's enough left for this tour. Now, we mix the white hard varnish with a little surgical spirit, don't we?

THE DRESSER

SIR: I know how to stick on a beard. I have been a depictor for over forty years and steered my own course for over thirty. You think I don't know how to affix a beard and moustache? You overstep the mark, boy. Don't get above yourself. *(SIR begins to apply the gum, and stick on the beard. NORMAN turns his back and has a nip of brandy)* I shall want a rest after the storm scene.

NORMAN: There's no need to tell me. I know.

SIR: Towel. *(NORMAN hands SIR a towel which SIR presses against the beard and moustache. SIR looks at himself in the looking-glass, and suddenly goes blank)* Something's missing. What's missing?

NORMAN: I don't want to get above myself, Sir, but how about the wig? *(NORMAN removes the wig from the block and hands it to SIR)* And shall we take extra care with the join tonight? On Tuesday Richard III looked as if he were wearing a peaked cap.

(SIR puts on the wig and begins to colour the join. HE stops—)

SIR: Hot, unbearably hot, going to faint—

(NORMAN whips out the brandy bottle)

NORMAN: Have a nip, it won't harm— *(SIR waves him away. NORMAN has a nip, puts the bottle away, and returns to SIR, who hasn't moved)* Oh, Sir, we mustn't give up, not now, not now. Let's highlight our lines.

(Silence. SIR continues to add highlights)

SIR: Imagine bombing the Grand Theatre, Plymouth. Barbarians. *(Pause)* I shall give them a good one tonight. *(Pause. SIR becomes alarmed)* Norman!

NORMAN: Sir?

SIR: What's the first line again? All this clitter-clatter-chitter-chatter—

NORMAN: 'Attend the Lords of France and Burgundy—'

SIR: You've put it from my head. You must keep silent when I'm dressing. I have to work to do, work, hard bloody labour, I have to carry the world tonight, the whole bloody universe—

NORMAN: Sir, Sir—

SIR: I can't remember the first line. A hundred thousand performances behind me and I have to ask you for the first line—

NORMAN: I'll take you through it—

SIR: Take me through it? Nobody takes you through it, you're put

113

through it, night after night, and I haven't the strength.

NORMAN: Well, you're a fine one, I must say, you of all people, you disappoint me, if you don't mind my saying so. You, who always say self-pity is the most unattractive quality on stage or off. Who have you been working for all these years? The Ministry of Information? Struggle and survival, you say, that's all that matters, you say, struggle and survival. Well, we all bloody struggle, don't we? I struggle, I struggle, you think it's easy for me, well, I'll tell you something for nothing it isn't easy, not one little bit, neither the struggle nor the bloody survival. The whole world's struggling for bloody survival, so why can't you?

(Silence)

SIR: My dear Norman, I seem to have upset you. I apologise. I understand. We cannot always be strong. There are dangers in covering the cracks.

NORMAN: Never mind about covering the cracks, what about the wig join?

(SIR continues to make up)

NORMAN: I'm sorry if I disturbed your concentration.

SIR: 'We both understand servitude, Alfonso.' What came next? What did I say to that?

NORMAN: 'Was it lack of ambition allowed me to endure what I have had to endure? It depends, your highness, what is meant by ambition. If ambition means a desire to sit in the seats of the mighty, yes, I have lacked such ambition. To me it has been a matter of some indifference where I have done my work. It has been the work itself which has been my chief joy.'

SIR: A fine memory, Norman.

NORMAN: My memory's like a policeman. Never there when you want it.

SIR: That was a play. And a money-maker. Greatly admired by clever charwomen and stupid clergymen. If I was twenty years younger I could still go on acting that kind of rubbish. But now I have to ascend the cosmos. And do they care? I hate the swines.

NORMAN: Shall we finish our eyebrows?

EASTERN STANDARD
by Richard Greenberg
NYC restaurant - Present - Drew (late 20's) - Stephen (30)

Stephen - An architect who despises his job
Drew - Stephen's gay friend

Six people meet in a restaurant in New York City and become
firends. Stephen falls in live with Phoebe, a Wall Street broker.
Drew is attracted to Phoebe's brother, Peter. Ellen, a waitress,
and May, a schizophrenic, street person, are drawn into the
group who gather at Stephen's summer home on Fire Island.
Here, Stephen and Drew have met in a restaurant to catch up on
each others' lives. Both are discontent and Stephen is waiting
for Phoebe, to whom he is attracted but has never met, to
arrive.

DREW: I can't believe I came this far uptown. And in broad daylight.
STEPHEN: Thank you for compromising your principles.
DREW: Well, the whole adolescent aspect of it was irresistible. I
can't think of anything more adorable than acting like we're nineteen
again and it's fall at Dartmouth—
STEPHEN: Well, whatever.
DREW: —and we're bivouacked for the season in front of some girl's
dorm room. And her name is Doe or Fauna and we're waiting for her
to emerge from the gloaming so she can ignore you or forget your
name. And I tell you it's unhealthy and you say you don't care, it's
enough to be in her vicinity—
STEPHEN: Well, those were desperate times-
DREW: And she finally does appear and whisks right past you, as if
you were air, but you're chasing her, anyway, which is hopeless. And
I should really be using my studio time to paint, but I'm there, too,
because *I'm* chasing *you*, which is worse than hopeless. Thank God
those days are over! *(Beat)* You're sure she's coming?
STEPHEN: Every lunch hour. Like clockwork.
DREW: Inexpressible lust between you like a tension rod, I love it—
STEPHEN: How are you?

115

DREW: Me?

STEPHEN: None other.

DREW: I've been better.

STEPHEN: I'm sorry.

DREW: Actually, something pretty rotten has happened.

STEPHEN: Tell me.

DREW: Well, it's the worst, actually.

STEPHEN: What do you mean? *(The waitress comes into view.)*

DREW: Do you want another? *(Stephen shakes his head "no.")* Oh, actress! *(The waitress looks at him.)* Another kir, please. *(She exits.)*

STEPHEN: What do you mean, the worst?

DREW: The worst. The worst that could happen to someone like me. In the course of my daily life.

STEPHEN: Drew—

DREW: Think about it. *(Beat.)*

STEPHEN: Oh God...

DREW: Yes.

STEPHEN: Oh, Jesus—

DREW: The maid. *(Beat.)*

STEPHEN: What?

DREW: She steals.

STEPHEN: The maid.

DREW: Steals—

STEPHEN: You asshole—

DREW: Cuff links, a goddamn Hermes tie—

STEPHEN: You asshole....you're such an—

DREW: I *trusted* her, Stephen. She was very nearly my most intimate relationship at this moment.

STEPHEN: I thought you were going to say you had—

DREW: She's been my maid for four years. She was the first maid I ever had. We were like *this*. *(Twines his fingers.)*

STEPHEN: You are disgustingly middle class.

DREW: Of course I am. What other class is open to me? But no one knows it because my painting is usually obscene. Does grouper tortellini sound as creative to you as it does to me? *(The waitress enters*

116

with Drew's drink.)
STEPHEN: Worse.
DREW: Then I *must* have it.
STEPHEN: So how did it go with Doug?
DREW: With—?
STEPHEN: Doug.
DREW: Doug. Doug—Doug—Doug...
STEPHEN: Doug—who—I—
DREW: Doug-who-you-introduced-me-too—yes! Doug-from-the-office-Doug.
STEPHEN: Yes.
DREW: Dull-as-dishwater-Doug.
STEPHEN: ...Oh.
DREW: Well, it didn't go all that well, actually.
STEPHEN: Too bad—
DREW: I *mean*—
STEPHEN: He seemed—
DREW: Really, Stephen. He's not handsome, he's not charming, he's not even rich, which at least would be *something*. He has many finer qualities, which don't interest me at *all*. I sit there thinking, has Stephen lost his mind?
STEPHEN: I just thought—
DREW: I could not figure out *what* you wre thinking. Suddenly, he leans over to me— We're in this bar, the god-help-me *Upper* East Side—he leans over to me and says, "I don't know if Stephen told you; I've never...blush, sigh, harrumph...*been* with a man before." All of a sudden I uncover your hidden agenda: this is a match made in hygiene! Stephen, please, you're very sweet, but—
STEPHEN: He seemed like your type.
DREW: Catatonic has never been my type, Stephen. The truth is, you think that when I broke up with Eric I embarked on a sexual rout of Manhattan Island. Well, I haven't, so why not give me a break? I wasn't having fun, so we broke up, big deal.
STEPHEN: You made no effort.
DREW: I don't *want* to make an effort! Why should everything be an

effort? God. He was...depressed. He was depressing. He put a damper on everything. I saw no utility in spending the charred remains of my youth on a bad time. Why am I justifying myself to you? You've been rebounded on more often than a basketball court, you're hardly the one to dispense advice on how to—oh, look, look, I'm getting all riled, I'm not going into this. So tell me-how are *you*? *(Beat.)*

STEPHEN: Fine.

DREW: Really? *(Beat.)*

STEPHEN: Well...fair...

DREW: What have you been doing? *(Beat.)*

STEPHEN: Nothing much. *(Beat.)* I swallowed a bottle of pills last night. *(Pause. The waitress enters with their tortellini.)* This tortellini looks disgusting.

DREW: Oh, Jesus...

STEPHEN: I mean, I don't even know how to *order*—

DREW: Stephen—Stephen—

STEPHEN: There's something nightmarish about not ever getting satisfaction in a restaurant.

DREW: *Will you goddamn tell me what you*—

STEPHEN: Lower your voice—it's a restaurant—

DREW: Will you goddamn it tell me what you—

STEPHEN: It was nothing.

DREW: Oh, right.

STEPHEN: It turned out to be nothing. I'm alive, I'm well; before the tortellini came, I wasn't even sick to my stomach—

DREW: Stephen—

STEPHEN: It was a whim; don't you ever have whims?

DREW: Yes; I usually end up buying shoes.

STEPHEN: I stuck my finger down my throat in plenty of time—

DREW: Why did you do this? It's so abnormal.

STEPHEN: I hate my job. All I get from it is money, which I've always had, and I hate it.

DREW: ...There are other ways to quit a job, Stephen.

STEPHEN: I walked down the street the other day and saw three buildings our firm designed. It was pitch black at high noon. I *am* urban blight.

DREW: Stephen, lots of people hate their jobs.

STEPHEN: It's so far beyond that, Drew. What I do...is evil. *(Beat.)*

DREW: It's not evil, Stephen; it's architecture.

STEPHEN: Do you know how this job works?

DREW: ...Vaguely.

STEPHEN: Okay. There's a parcel of land somewhere in a neighborhood that's changing. A developer wants it, only there's a tenement there. Twelve welfare families. No problem, there's a slumlord, he gets to work. Small, inexplicable fires, no heat in February, hired thugs. One missed rent payment, they're out on the street. What happens to them? Drugs, prostitution, crime—I don't have to know, it preceded my involvement, it doesn't apply to me.

DREW: Yes, there's a certain amount of equivocating involved, I—

STEPHEN: Fine. So now the developer has his land, he comes to us, and says, "Make me a building, I don't care what it looks like as long as people notice it." Then, because the firm is so diversified and I'm doing so well, my boss comes to me. "Stephen, I'd really like your input on this." I get to work. I come up with a rough design. It's harmonious, it's contextual, it's functional, it's tasteful. It's not risky— that comes later when I go independent—but it's nothing to be ashamed of, either.

DREW: Well, there you—

STEPHEN: The boss sees it, says, "Excellent! Really fine work. Only guess what? We're adding twenty stories." "Twenty stories?" I say. "But if we add twenty more stories, this building will look more or less as if it's *eating* the rest of the block. Besides this neighborhood isn't zoned for twenty more stories." "The builder got a variance," I'm told. "He promised to re-decorate the subway." "Oh," I say, dumbstruck as ever by the tortuous path of bureaucratic concessions. And all of a sudden, this monstrosity is going up. It's uglier than sin, it blocks the light from East Thirty-Fourth Street to West Seventy-Second Street, and nobody wants to move into it because there's been such rampant over-development that nobody's moved into the last

119

twenty buildings exactly like it either. And I say to myself, "Stephen, you have labored mightily and brought forth an abortion. But, don't despair! For with any luck, this building will someday be demolished." Which means that everything I do is pardonable only insofar as it is potentially *reversible*. *(Beat.)* I don't know... Maybe if I had a girlfriend... *(Beat.)* When I went into this, I wanted... *(Long pause.)*

DREW: Well, you wanted something, Stephen, fine, I'm willing to concede that—

STEPHEN: And this is all I have. I don't have anything else. *(Beat.)* I was lying in bed—in the middle of the night—wide awake, as usual—and I went to the bathroom for my usual pill. And when I reached for the bottle, I realized that I was physically capable of swallowing all of its contents. Which was interesting. And then, I thought, no, of course I'll never do it—it's too abnormal. But then I thought—what's stopping me? Nothing. Which was also interesting. And then I did it. Which was fascinating. And I went back to bed and just lay there, waiting for the effects to start. And I realized that if I didn't do anything to reverse my actions, I would die. Which was *amazingly* interesting. And then all of a sudden, it came to me—this revelation—this flash of insight—this profound understanding—I can't kill myself, what would my parents think? And I stuck my finger down my throat.

DREW: *(Suppressing a smile.)* ...Not really?

STEPHEN: I'm thirty and I still have parents. If that isn't an admission of failure, I don't know what— *(Drew is laughing.)* What? *(Drew keeps laughing.)* What? *(He starts laughing too.)* Oh, god... *(They quiet down.)*

DREW: I'm sorry.

STEPHEN: No, it's—

DREW: I *am* sorry— *(Beat.)*

[WOMAN'S VOICE: *(At table, R.)* Goddamn it to hell!]

STEPHEN: What the hell is that?

DREW: *(Looks R., beyond the empty table.)* That's so *peculiar!*

STEPHEN: What? *(He shifts to follow Drew's gaze.)* Oh my God. Who *is* that?

DREW: I can't imagine.

EASTERN STANDARD

STEPHEN: This is really too much. The whole city's having a nervous breakdown.

DREW: Stephen—it's all right, she's quiet now. The waitress has taken care of it.

STEPHEN: Do you think I could *whine* a little more? I don't think I'm *whining* quite enough. *(Beat.)* She's not usually this late.

DREW: Tell me about her.

STEPHEN: We—well, it's stupid.

DREW: You've seen her every day for three weeks running.

STEPHEN: Almost every day. Almost three weeks.

DREW: And there's somethng between you?

STEPHEN: We've never spoken, we've...Christ, it's ridiculous.

DREW: You've never spoken?

STEPHEN: No.

DREW: Then, Stephen, if I may be so bold—it's not a real relationship.

STEPHEN: Of course it's not a real relationship! I don't *have* real relationships. I place myself beside emotionally teetering women and wait for them to fall on me. I share jangled nerves with neurotics for short spans of time...it's preposterous, I'm a preposterous figure—

DREW: She's beautiful.

STEPHEN: She's all I've been able to think about—

DREW: Stephen—

STEPHEN: It's like I'm nineteen, I'm obsessed, I follow her...I follow her places...she doesn't know...I stare...I nod, I smile, I *scrape*... Nothing will come of it, nothing will ever come of it, it will just end up making me more miserable than ever. Why can't I control myself? *Where is she?*

DREW: Stephen—

STEPHEN: Shoot me, take that knife and run it through my heart. *(Phoebe enters, sees Stephen's back, smiles to herself, takes seat at table, L.C.)*

DREW: Stephen?

STEPHEN: What?

DREW: Is that her? *(Stephen whips around to look at her, whips back*

121

quickly.)
STEPHEN: Oh, Jesus.
DREW: Do you always twist so violently when you see her?
STEPHEN: Yes.
DREW: That may be a flaw in your strategy. My, my...
STEPHEN: How does she look to you?
DREW: Fiscal.
STEPHEN: Drew!
DREW: No, this is incredible; I have never seen anyone so ambient of Wall Street in my life. She looks as if she breakfasts on ticker tape and the Dow rises with her hemline, she's your Platonic half, oh, Stephen, lunge!
STEPHEN: Would you lower your voice, we're in a restaurant.
DREW: She can't hear me. *(The waitress brings her a drink; they smile, nod; waitress exists.)* Oh my God!
STEPHEN: What?
DREW: The waitress just brought her a white wine. She didn't even ask for it, now that's classy—would you relax your back, you look like a porcupine.
STEPHEN: I should never have asked you to come, I can see that.
DREW: I'm just having some fun—I absolutely approve.
STEPHEN: There's nothing to approve of.
DREW: Well, there may be. *(Peter enters, kisses Phoebe on the cheek, sits by her; they begin to talk, all of this inaudible to us.)* Oh my God! *(Drew starts up out of his chair, staring at Peter.)*
STEPHEN: What?
DREW: Oh my God!
STEPHEN: Would you please sit down?
DREW: God, that's beautiful.
STEPHEN: What are you talking about?
DREW: It's what the Garden of Eden must have looked like.
STEPHEN: What?
DREW: The two of them together.
STEPHEN: There's a man with her?
DREW: Yes. A beautiful one.

STEPHEN: There's never been before. *(Peter lights a cigarette.)*

DREW: Thank you for asking me here.

STEPHEN: How can there be a man? She always eats alone.

DREW: They're like perfect reflecting pools, God, it's—

STEPHEN: I want to die.

DREW: Their children will be *incredible!*

STEPHEN: Children! Oh god—!

DREW: Stephen—

STEPHEN: I'm an idiot! *(Beat.)*

DREW: Listen, Stephen. In a couple of weeks, it'll be summer. We'll go to your place on the Island. We'll get out of the city, okay? It's just the city. Forget about her. Okay? Forget about her. It's silly. Everything will be fine.

THE END OF I
by Diana Amsterdam
A country road at night - Present - Jerome (30-40) - Curtis (30-40)

Jerome - A man fighting his fear of death
Curtis - Jerome's friend, a teacher

Jerome and Curtis are old motorcycling buddies who keep meeting on a particularly dangerous mountain road long after their riding skills have begun to wane. Here, the two contemplate the possibility of attempting to ride the treacherous pass one last time.

(Nightime. A country road. A full MOON. CRICKETS. Before the LIGHTS rise, JEROME and CURTIS shout, overlapping:)
JEROME: Wee-haw! Start 'er up! Let's go! Open 'er up!
CURTIS: All right! Here we go! Away! Let 'er rip! Charge!
(The lights rise on JEROME and CURTIS sitting on their motorcycles. THEY are leaning forward in a posture of eager anticipation as if they're just about to take off. Overlapping:)
JEROME: Eeeh-hee! Here we go! Fuck, let's mix 'er up! Go! Go! Go!
CURTIS: Woo-hoo! Charge! Charge! Move! Go! Go! Go go go go!
(NEITHER MAN moves.)
CURTIS: It's not working.
JEROME: It will.
CURTIS: I think we lost it, I think we really lost it.
JEROME: If we lost it, we can find it.
CURTIS: We've been sitting her for, God, almost an hour, look, if I don't get home soon, Pammy'll kill me.
JEROME: Pammy! Where does Pammy keep your balls since she cut them off?
CURTIS: That's not like you.
(JEROME takes out a flask.)
CURTIS: What's that?
JEROME: Apple juice.

THE END OF I

CURTIS: You're not going to start drinking now?

JEROME: Damn right I am.

CURTIS: You think I'm gonna ride with you plastered?

JEROME: You used to ride with me plastered, you used to ride with me blottoed, you used to ride with me upside down.

CURTIS: That was before—

JEROME: Don't mention it—

CURTIS: Before—

JEROME: Don't talk about it!

CURTIS: Put that thing away. If you don't put that thing away, Jerome Corsky, you won't be riding this hill tonight.

JEROME: Don't talk to me in your goddamn teacher voice, you're not in any goddamn classroom now. *(Puts away flask.)* Okay, damnit! Wee-haw! Shit!, let 'er ride! Ride! Ride!

CURTIS: Okay! Out we go! In we go! On we go! Over we go! *(THEY don't move.)*

CURTIS: We lost it.

(During the following, CURTIS lags behind Jerome, but catches up with increasing vigor.)

JEROME:	CURTIS:
I, Jerome Corsky, do hereby pledge, to my bike When I'm with you I won't hurry I won't worry	Come on. I don't remember it. That was when we had twenty-five guys... When I. Curtis Spoonfellow. Do hereby pledge to my bike When I'm with you I won't hurry I won't worry I won't hurry I won't worry
I won't think what could be I won't think what would be All I'm gonna do is Ride	I won't think what would be I won't think what could be *(Correcting himself.)* would be—

125

THE END OF I

I won't judge
I won't fudge
I won't coddle no boss

I won't regret no loss
All I'm gonna do is
Ride
I won't look back
I won't detract
All I'm gonna do is
All I'm gonna do is
Ride
And when I ride,
I'm gonna ride high,
Touch the sky,
With my pals by my
side,
I'm gonna fly free
This road and me.
I, Jerome Corsky,
Do hereby pledge
I'm gonna
Ride!

(Catching up.)
All I'm gonna do is
Ride
I won't judge I won't
fudge I won't coddle no boss
regret no loss
All I'm gonna do is
Ride
I won't look back
I won't detract
All I'm gonna do is
All I'm gonna do is
Ride
And when I ride,
I'm gonna ride high,
Touch the sky,
My pals by my side,
I'm gonna fly free
This road and me.
I, Curtis Spoonfellow,
Do hereby pledge
I'm gonna Ride!

(THEY end on a upbeat, obviously exhilarated.)
JEROME: Goddamn that can still do it, I should've been a poet, Curtis, I should've been a goddamn poet.
CURTIS: You're a poet, Jerry, you really are. By the way, it's "this road and I"...
JEROME: What?
CURTIS: In the pledge. If you want to be a poet, it's not correct to say "this road and *me*," it's "this road and *I*."
JEROME: That doesn't rhyme.
CURTIS: Yeah, but it could, see, just take out the "free," just make a little change—
JEROME: I don't want to make a little change. Who the hell wants

to make a little change?

CURTIS: The rules of good grammar—

JEROME: Fuck!...the rules of good grammar. What has happened to you? What the hell has happened to you? What has happened to all of us? What the hell has happened to all of us?

CURTIS: You know what happened—

JEROME: Don't mention it—

CURTIS: You gotta want to talk about it—

(Viciously, JEROME starts up his MOTORCYCLE. CURTIS takes the cue and starts his MOTORCYCLE. THEY sit there, revving their MOTORCYCLES. CURTIS turns off this MOTORCYCLE. After quite awhile, JEROME turns off his MOTORCYCLE.)

CURTIS: We lost it.

JEROME: Must you keep saying that?

CURTIS: Look, why don't we just pack up, put the bikes back on the truck, go home, have a beer, maybe stop for a beer, okay? All the other guys dropped out long ago, even before—

JEROME: Don't mention it!

CURTIS: Even before Marty—

JEROME: Don't mention it, I tell you!

CURTIS: Don't you want to talk about it?

JEROME: Not here. Not now.

CURTIS: Okay, not here, not now, then let's make a date— *(Takes out his appointment book.)* What's good for you? I'm free two days this week after school, no, wait, Thursday I have to take Glinda to the dentist, Friday might be good if we can do it close, wait, or at least halfway between—

(JEROME jumps off his bike, and grabs Curtis' appointment book.)

CURTIS: Hey!

JEROME: You bring your appointment book with you on the bike?

CURTIS: You bring your whiskey.

JEROME: Whiskey belongs with motorcycles, appointment books belong with goddamn briefcases!

CURTIS: That's in the truck. Look, I thought I might have time on the way home, I'd check my lesson plans, if you're driving, what's wrong with that—

JEROME: We're here on the mountain! You forgot what it means to be here on the mountain on our bikes?

(THEY are both silent for a moment. The sound of the CRICKETS is very loud. JEROME returns Curtis's book.)

JEROME: Curt. If we don't ride soon, you know we're never gonna ride again. Tick tick tick one by one you do everything for the last time. You ride for the last time. You make love for the last time. You breathe for the last time. And you don't even know it. Are you ready to say you've ridden for the last time?

CURTIS: Well, I'd sure rather ride for the last time than breathe for the last time.

JEROME: *(Overlapping.)* You're missing my whole point.

CURTIS: I think I got your whole point.

JEROME: My point is that you've got to guard against this creeping last-timism, you can't let it get you—

CURTIS: You're talking about Marty, that's who you're talking about, you're talking about Marty, Marty—

JEROME: *(Shouts.)* I am not talking about Marty! Damn you! Curt. I'm sorry. I know I've been an unbelievable shit lately—

CURTIS: You really have—

JEROME: Because I haven't been getting any sleep, I've been so worried about—about everything, but I'm not ready to say I'm never going to ride again. Are you?

CURTIS: I don't know. Maybe I am. Why should we of everybody, of the whole gang, be the last ones out here? I mean I could make, next year I could make assistant principal, when the Russian delegation came to my school, they came to *my* classroom. Mine. TV camera and all. I learned how to say "zdrastvuge." Hello. What would the Russian delegation think if they knew I was up here riding tonight?

JEROME: What the hell do you care what the Russian delegation thinks?

CURTIS: It's just that you can't help noticing the enormous disparity, the gulf, even, between what the Russian delegation thinks of me and me here on this bike—

THE END OF I

JEROME: Fuck! I'll tell you what the Russian delegation would think, I'll tell you what the Russian delegation would think, they'd think, look at that bitchin' machine, jeezus, I wish I had me a machine like that baby, that's what they'd think.

CURTIS: They would never use the word "bitchin'."

JEROME: For Chrissake—

CURTIS: I met them!

JEROME: Curtis. Don't fail me. Don't fail me, buddy. You and me—

CURTIS: I.

JEROME: You and I were riding before the rest of 'em. Remember the thrill. Taking a curve like it was inside your own spine, you forget to think, you just move, time stops but you're still moving like a goddamn tiger pure reflex. It's so good. Please. Let's give it one more chance. Please. Tomorrow night, same place same time.

CURTIS: Tomorrow night? *(Checks appointment book.)* Maybe tomorrow night, no, not tomorrow night, I promised Pammy I'd help her with the pastry crust for the big dinner party, I have it right here, *(Shows book.)*, "crust"—

JEROME: Please!

CURTIS: Her manager will be there. Not that she has a manager, she doesn't really have a manager, I mean she *has* a manager, but the manger couldn't manage without Pammy...

JEROME: Please! Buddy!

CURTIS: Okay, buddy. *(Takes a fancy fountain pen set from his leather jacket pocket, makes an insertion in his appointment book.)* Wednesday October twelve. Ride with Jerry on Crystal Mountain. Could we make it nine-fifteen? *(LIGHTS down.)*

HURLYBURLY
by David Rabe
Los Angeles - Present - Phil (30's) - Eddie (30's)

Phil - An actor
Eddie - A casting agent

Following a particularly violent argument with his wife, Phil
travels to the home of his good griend, Eddie in search of
comfort.   Eddie, who is suffering from a coke hangover,
provides the necessary companionship and the two self-absorbed
men fan the flames of one another's misogyny.

PHIL: Eddie!
EDDIE: *(startled, sitting up)* WHAT? *(As PHIL tosses the newspaper
onto EDDIE's lap.)*
PHIL: Eddie, you awake or not?
EDDIE: *(Disoriented, he bolts to his feet and stands there.)* I don't
know. How about you?
PHIL: *(taking off his sunglasses, sticking them in his jacket pocket)*
Eddie, I'm standin' here. How you doin'?
EDDIE: I don't know. Did I leave the door open?
PHIL: It was open.
EDDIE: *(A man in command, almost bragging, he staggers to the
door, shutting it, and then comes wandering back toward the couch,
carrying the newspaper with him, dragging his trousers along behind
him.)* I come home last night, I was feelin' depressed. I sat around,
I watched some TV. Somebody called and hung up when I answered.
I smoked some dope, took a couple of ludes. The TV got to look very
good. It was a bunch of shit, but it looked very good due to the dope
and due to the ludes. *(Dropping the newspaper on the end table beside
the couch, he turns off the T.V. using the remote control and sags onto
the couch.)* So I musta fell asleep at some point. *(He is sinking back
as if he might go back to sleep.)*
PHIL: *(Poking EDDIE again to make sure he wakes up, PHIL heads
for the kitchen, as EDDIE sits back up.)* Maybe I'll make us some
coffee. Where is everything? By the stove and stuff?

EDDIE: *(sitting back up)* What time is it?

PHIL: It's over.

EDDIE: What?

PHIL: Everything.

EDDIE: *(Rising, staggering toward the kitchen, his trousers dragging along by the ankle, he is a little irritated that PHIL is bothering him in this way.)* What EVERYTHING?

PHIL: Me and Susie.

EDDIE: Whata you mean, "everything"? *(At the sink, EDDIE soaks a towel.)*

PHIL: Everything. The whole thing. You know. Our relationship. I really fucked up this time. I really did. *(PHIL rattles the tea kettle to find that there is water in it, then sets it on the stove which he turns on.)*

EDDIE: You had a fight. So what? Give her a little time and call her up, you know that. Don't be so goddamn negative.

PHIL: This was a big one.

EDDIE: Bigger than the last one?

PHIL: Yeah.

EDDIE: So what'd you do, shoot her? *(He starts away toward the living room. Silence, as PHIL is preparing the instant coffee in the cups. EDDIE freezes, whirls back.)* You didn't shoot her, Phil. You got a gun?

PHIL: On me? *(Patting his jacket pockets he pulls out a silver, chrome-plated, snub-nosed .38.)*

EDDIE: You didn't shoot her, Phil.

PHIL: No.

EDDIE: *(He heads back toward the couch, taking his towel and a bottle of aspirin with him.)* So, she'll take you back. She always takes you back.

PHIL: I went too far. She ain't going to take me back.

EDDIE: You want me to call her?

PHIL: She'll give you the fucking business. She hates you.

EDDIE: *(irritated that PHIL should even say such a thing)* What are you talking about, she hates me? Susie don't hate me. She likes me.

PHIL: She hates you. She tol' me. In the middle of the fight.

EDDIE: *(his head killing him, he takes some aspirin)* What are you talking about: you two are in the middle of this bloodbath—the goddamn climactic go-round of your three-year career in, you know what I mean, marital carnage and somewhere in the peak of this motherfucker she takes time out to tell you she hates good ol' Eddie. Am I supposed to believe that?

PHIL: *(As PHIL, bringing a can of beer, joins EDDIE on the couch.)* I was surprised too. I thought she liked you.

EDDIE: You're serious.

PHIL: Yeah.

EDDIE: Fuck her—what a whore! She acted like she liked me.

PHIL: I thought she liked me.

EDDIE: I thought she liked you, too. I mean, she don't like anybody, is that the situation, the pathetic bitch? *(Leaping to his feet, he heads for the stairway to the second floor, kicking off his trousers as he goes.)*

PHIL: I knew she hated Artie.

EDDIE: I knew she hated Artie, too. But Artie's an abnoxious, anal obsessive pain in the ass who could make his best friend hire crazed, unhappy people with criminal tendencies to cut off his legs, which we have both personally threatened to do. So that proves nothing. *(As he is about to Enter the bathroom, he pauses to look down at PHIL.)* I mean, what the hell does she think gives her justification to hate me?

PHIL: *(He drifts toward the base of the stairs, looking up.)* She didn't say.

EDDIE: *(He freezes where he stands.)* She didn't say?

PHIL: No.

EDDIE: *(bolting into the bathroom, he yells on from within it)* I mean, did she have a point of reference, some sort of reference from within your blowup out of which she made some goddamn association which was for her justification that she come veering off to dump all this unbelievable vituperative horseshit over me—whatever it was. I wanna get it straight. *(Toilet is flushed within the bathroom.)*

PHIL: You got some weed? I need some weed. *(On the base of the stairs, as Eddie emerges from the bathroom, pulling on a pair of raggedy, cut off gym pants as he heads down the stairs.)*

EDDIE: So what'd she say about me? You know, think back. So the two of you are hurling insults and she's a bitch, blah, blah, blah, you're a bastard, rapateta. *(Picking up the dope box from the hassock, he is about to go to the couch.)* So in the midst of this TUMULT where do I come in?

PHIL: You're just like me, she says.

EDDIE: What? *(He stops; can't believe it.)* We're alike? She said that?

PHIL: Yeah—we were both whatever it was she was calling me at the time.

EDDIE: *(Flopping down on the arm of the chair, he hands PHIL a joint.)* I mean, that's sad. She's sad. They're all sad. They're all fucking pathetic. What is she thinking about?

PHIL: I don't know.

EDDIE: What do you think she's thinking about?

PHIL: We're friends. You know. So she thinks we got somethin' in common. It's logical.

EDDIE: But we're friends on the basis of what, Phil? On the basis of opposites, right? We're totally dissimilar is the basis of our friendship, right?

PHIL: Of course. *(As the tea kettle whistles, PHIL heads for the kitchen, EDDIE following.)*

EDDIE: I mean, I been her friend longer than I been yours. What does she think, that I've been—what? More sympathetic to you than her in these goddamn disputes you two have? If that's what she thought she should have had the guts to tell me, confront me! *(Having dug a second joint from the dope box, he heads back for the couch now, leaving the box on the counter, as PHIL pours the hot water into the coffee cups and stirs them.)*

PHIL: I don't think that's what she thought.

EDDIE: SO WHAT WAS IT?

PHIL: I don't know. I don't think she thinks.

EDDIE: None of them think, I don't know what they do.

PHIL: They don't think. *(Carrying the two cups, he heads for the*

couch and EDDIE.)
EDDIE: They express their feelings. I mean, my feelings are hurt, too.
PHIL: Mine, too.
EDDIE: This is terrible on a certain level. I mean, I liked you two together.
PHIL: I know. Me, too. A lot of people did. I'm very upset. Let me have some more weed. *(Reaching back he grabs the joint from EDDIE.)* It was terrible. It was somethin'. Blah-blah-blah!
EDDIE: Rapateta. Hey, absolutely. *(sagging back onto the couch, lying back to rest, the towel on his forehead)*
PHIL: Blah-blah-blah! You know, I come home in the middle 'a the night—she was out initially with her girlfriends, so naturally I was alone and went out too. So I come home, I'm ripped, I was on a tear, but I'm harmless, except I'm on a talking jag, you know, who cares? She could have some sympathy for the fact that I'm ripped, she could take that into consideration, let me run my mouth a little, I'll fall asleep, where's the problem? That's what you would do for me, right?
EDDIE: Yeah.
PHIL: She can't do that.
EDDIE: What's she do? What the hell's the matter with her, she can't do that?
PHIL: *(Rising, a little agitated, he takes off his coat, tosses it onto the arm chair, pacing a little.)* I'm on a tear, see, I got a theory how to take Las Vegas and turn it upside down like it's a little rich kid and shake all the money out of its pockets, right?
EDDIE; Yeah. So what was it?
PHIL: It was bullshit, Eddie. *(sitting back down opposite EDDIE)* I was demented and totally ranting, so to that extent she was right to pay me no attention, seriously, but she should of faked it. But she not only sleeps, she snores. So I gotta wake her up, because, you know, the most important thing to me is that, in addition to this Las Vegas scam, I have this theory on the Far East, you know; it's a kind of vision of Global Politics, how to effect a real actual balance of power. She keeps interrupting me. You know, I'm losing my train of thought everytime

she interrupts me. It's a complex fucking idea, so I'm asking her to just have some consideration until I get the whole thing expressed, then she wants to have a counterattack, I couldn't be more ready.

EDDIE: She won't do that?

PHIL: No.

EDDIE: That's totally uncalled for, Phil. All you're asking for is civilization, right? You talk and she talks. That's civilization, right? You take turns!

PHIL: I don't think I'm asking for anything unusual, but I don't get it.

EDDIE: Perverse.

PHIL: Perverse is what she wrote the book on it. I am finally going totally crazy. *(jumping back up on his feet)* I've totally lost track of my ideas. I'm like lookin' into this hole in which was my ideas. I arrive thinkin' I can take Vegas and save the world. Forty-five seconds with her and I don't know what I'm talking about. So I tell her— "LISTEN!-lemme think a second, I gotta pick up the threads." She says some totally irrelevant but degrading shit about my idea and starts some nitpicking with which she obviously intends to undermine my whole fucking Far Eastern theory on the balance of powers, and I'm sayin', "Wait a minute," but she won't. So WHACK! I whack her one in the face. Down she goes.

EDDIE: You whacked her.

PHIL: I whacked her good. You see my hand. *(Moving away from EDDIE, PHIL holds his hand out behind him.)*

EDDIE: *(leaning forward a little to look at PHIL's hand)* You did that to your hand?

PHIL: Her fuckin' tooth, see.

EDDIE: You were having this political discussion with which she disagreed, so you whacked her out, is that right?

PHIL: *(He flops down on the hassock, smoking the dope.)* It wasn't the politics. I didn't say it was the politics.

EDDIE: What was it? *(Moving to PHIL, EDDIE hands PHIL his coffee.)*

PHIL: I don't know. I had this idea and then it was gone.

EDDIE: Yeah. *(Pacing behind PHIL, thinking, seeming to almost interrogate him.)*

PHIL: It was just this disgusting cloud like fucking with me and I went crazy.

EDDIE: Right. Whata you mean?

PHIL: You know this fog, and I was in it and it was talking to me with her face on it. Right in front of me was like this cloud with her face on it, but it wasn't just her, but this cloud saying all these mean things about my ideas and everything about me, so I was like shit and this cloud knew it. That was when it happened.

EDDIE: You whacked her.

PHIL: Yeah.

EDDIE: Was she all right?

PHIL: She was scared, and I was scared. I don't know if I was yelling I would kill her or she was yelling she was going to kill me.

EDDIE: Somebody was threatening, somebody, though.

PHIL: Definitely.

EDDIE: *(Settling down on the edge of the armchair behind Phil, EDDIE puts his arm around PHIL.)* So try and remember. Was it before you whacked her or after you whacked her that she made her reference to me?

PHIL: You mean that she hated you?

EDDIE: Yeah.

PHIL: Before. It was in the vicinity of Vegas, I think, but it gets blurry.

EDDIE: *(thoughtfully returning to the couch: he has his answer now)* So what musta happened is she decided I had some connection to your Vegas scam and this was for her justification to dump all this back-stabbing hostility all over me.

PHIL: She didn't say that. She just says we're both assholes.

EDDIE: But it would be logical that if this petty, cheap-shot animosity was in the vicinity of Vegas, it would have to do with Vegas. THAT WOULD ONLY BE LOGICAL.

PHIL: EXCEPT THAT SHE AIN'T LOGICAL. *(He is headed to join EDDIE who seems to have gotten things wrong.)*

EDDIE: True.

PHIL: *(sitting down on the couch)* SHE'S JUST A NASTY BITCH AND I MARRIED HER.

EDDIE: You know what I think?

PHIL: What?

EDDIE: She hates men.

PHIL: Whata you mean?

EDDIE: She hates you, she hates me. She hates men. I don't know what else to think. It's a goddamn syllogism. Susie hates Phil, Susie hates Eddie.

PHIL: And Artie, too.

EDDIE: Artie, Eddie, Phil are men, she hates men. The fucker's irrefutable, except that's not how it works, GODDAMNIT. *(Angrily, grabbing his glasses from the coffee table he heads to the dictionary lying atop the record players)*

PHIL: What?

EDDIE: You go from the general to the particular. I'm talking about a syllogism, here.

PHIL: Yeah.

EDDIE: *(Irritated, he paces behind the couch, leafing through the dictionary.)* Dammit! What the hell goes the other way?

PHIL: Which way?

EDDIE: Something goes the other goddamn way!

PHIL: What?

EDDIE: *(Pacing back and forth, he comes around the couch.)* You start from the particular in something. Susie hates Eddie, Susie hates Phil. Phil and Eddie are men, therefore, blah, blah, blah... Oh, my god, do you know what it is? *(sitting on the couch)*

PHIL: What?

EDDIE: Science! What goes the other way is science, in which you see all the shit like data and go from it to the law. *(Slamming shut the dictionary, he sets it on the end table, his glasses on top of it.)* This is even better. We have just verified, and I mean scientifically, the bitch has been proven to basically hate all men. She doesn't need a reason to hate me in particular—she already hates me in the fucking abstract. *(Upstairs, the toilet flushes and EDDIE stands, looking up at the bathroom.)*

PHIL: You gonna call her?

EDDIE: You want me to? I will if you want me to. *(He is rushing up the stairs.)*

PHIL: You said you were gonna!

EDDIE: That was before I understood the situation. Now that I understand the situation, the hell with her. The bitch wants to go around hating me in the fucking abstract! Are you nuts? Call her? *(Having reached the bathroom door, he pounds on it. He pounds and pounds.)* I wouldn't piss on her if the flames were about to engulf her goddamn, you know, central nervous system! *(As MICKEY staggers out of the bathroom onto the balcony heading to reach into his own room and grab a robe from off the door.)*

INFINITY'S HOUSE
by Ellen McLaughlin
Desert - 1945 - Oppenheimer - Rabi - (late 20's-early 40's)

Oppenheimer - A subtle and brilliant physicist
Rabi - Oppenheimer's equal and his only real friend

Two physicists who have helped to build the first atomic bomb
stand at the test site and discuss the implications of what they
have created.

(Slight drizzle. OPPENHEIMER and RABI walk on with umbrellas.)
OPPENHEIMER: If I was a betting man? Oh, I'd have to say chances
aren't great.
RABI: Seriously now. It's just me you're talking to. Don't you think
the chances are very good, in fact, that it will work?
OPPENHEIMER: I've lost all the perspective I ever had, which wasn't
that much. It's been like this *(HE puts his flattened hand, palm toward
him, an inch from his face)*, for months now. All I know is that if this
doesn't work after all this, the army will string me up as the Commie
they always knew I was. They'd love to do that, you know, they've
never liked me, they've always hated the fact that Groves picked me to
head the place.
RABI: Groves has more on the ball than most people give him credit
for. Hiring you was brilliant.
OPPENHEIMER: Groves knows exactly what he's doing, always, and
he always gets what he wants. *(RABI takes out a cigarette, but can't
find matches. OPPENHEIMER offers a light.)* Groves thinks I'm going
to crack up.
RABI: I know. That's why I'm here. *(THEY look at each other.)*
Groves asked me to come. I was sent for. Just like Rosencrantz and
what's-his-name.
OPPENHEIMER: Guildenstern. So what did he want you to do? See
if I knew a hawk from a handsaw?
RABI: Oh, Robert, I wanted to come anyway. You know Groves. He
was just looking after you. He thought you should have friends about.
OPPENHEIMER: He thinks I'm nuts.

INFINITY'S HOUSE

RABI: Are you? *(Pause.)*

OPPENHEIMER: Do I seem crazy to you?

RABI: No. Well, yes, actually, a little. But then new truths always jog reality a bit. Don't you think? It's always seemed to me that going crackers is just an occupational hazard for physicists. And you combine with that what it is you are in fact *doing*—you'd be crazy *not* to feel crazy. What was it Bohr used to say—"Is it crazy enough to be right?"

OPPENHEIMER: Yes. Bohr was always very clear on that, that the real discoveries always seem totally insane when they're first proposed. I think that's why they're so beautiful.

RABI: And when you think of it—well, the whole idea of space being curved, for instance, it's literally unthinkable.

OPPENHEIMER: Exactly. I still remember when I first heard that. I came home from the library when I was, I think, fourteen, thirteen or fourteen, and I'd just read that the universe was finite, that space was curved and thus inclusive. Suddenly that whole, you know, that lovely childish notion that when you look out at a night sky, space goes on for ever and ever—I suppose it's comforting—that beautiful idea of infinity, but it had shattered for me that afternoon. Bleak New York twilight, and I came home, it was cold, and I just sat down at our dining-room table, I didn't bother taking off my coat or hat, I just sat there, dazedly staring at this bowl of oranges on the table, and I kept trying to imagine this curved lump of a universe and it kept becoming an orange, nice and finite and round and false, sitting there in space, with a context, you know, and I couldn't manage an image of this universe. It was the first time my mind had failed me, my visual imagination. And I realized it would always fail me where truth was concerned, and that I had reached a threshold of some kind and had become a theoretician.

RABI: Yes. From the first it's a matter of giving up a level of rationality that allows us to function in the world.

OPPENHEIMER: There's a Zen saying that the search for truth is like riding an ox in search of an ox.

RABI: *(Spotting a book in OPPENHEIMER'S pocket)* Oh my God, they were right. *(HE picks OPPENHEIMER'S pocket of a book.)* Ah ha, they were right. Well, well, well, I must say, Robert, bringing the

INFINITY'S HOUSE

<u>Bhagavad-Gita</u> to the test site of all places—

OPPENHEIMER: It helps.

RABI: Isn't is subtitled "Krishna's Counsel in Time of War"—?

OPPENHEIMER: —Subtitled?—

RABI: —Well, that explains it. Krishna basically says, "Go for it," doesn't he?

OPPENHEIMER: Well...

RABI: He appears to some prince—I'm not a complete philistine—he appears to some prince—

OPPENHEIMER: —Prince Arjuna.

RABI: The guy is on a battlefield, preparing for a war he doesn't want to fight, and Krishna says, "Stop feeling guilty and just go out and kill." Right?

OPPENHEIMER: Yes. And <u>Moby Dick</u> is a book about a whale.

RABI: Well, it is, isn't it?

OPPENHEIMER: I suppose.

RABI: You find this comforting?

OPPENHEIMER: I didn't say it was comforting. It helps. Yes, ostensibly, it's about Krishna convincing Arjuna to fight a battle against his kin, which he doesn't want to do, but the counsel is really about disciplining the mind away from worldly attachment, the process of purifying oneself spiritually to render oneself capable of detached action.

RABI: Uh huh.

OPPENHEIMER: And there're some uncanny passages in it—I don't know how well you know it—

RABI: College. No, not very well.

OPPENHEIMER: Oh. Well, then, I'll show you. *(HE lights his lighter, and reads from the book)* Well, um, yes, here...Arjuna asks... ah, he says, "If you think I can behold you in your cosmic form, reveal yourself," well, more like, "Reveal your immutable self, Krishna, Lord of Discipline..."

RABI: This isn't already translated?

OPPENHEIMER: No, well, this is the Sanskrit.

RABI: Uh huh.

INFINITY'S HOUSE

OPPENHEIMER: And, you remember Krishna has been disguised all this time as Arjuna's charioteer. So he finally presents himself in his real majesty as a huge, well, sun, I guess you could say.

RABI: Really?

OPPENHEIMER: "If the light of hundreds and thousands of suns were to rise in the sky at once it would be like the light of that great spirit." And Arjuna says, "I see everything contained in you, the past, the present and the future...I see all the gods assembled at once in your body, O Lord, and all of life, every living creature born and unborn blazes within you now. I see your infinite presence everywhere"—this isn't, it's better than this, I'm just—

RABI: It's fine, go on.

OPPENHEIMER: "Your infinite presence is everywhere, your countless arms, bellies, mouths and eyes, Lord of all, I can see in you no end or middle or beginning...um...I think you are man's timeless spirit...the ultimate, the still center of the spinning multitudes...your, your brilliance scorches the universe and the very planets behold you with awe...your blinding majesty licks the clouds with flames of countless colors, your mouths are open, gaping, your vast eyes burn through all creation. I quake and I can find no end to my terror at this sight. As moths in the frenzy of destruction fly in a blazing flame, worlds in the frenzy of destruction enter your mouths. In all directions I am bewildered... Tell me, who are you in this terrible form?" And Krishna says, "I am become Death, shatterer of worlds." And Arjuna says, "O God, O Krishna, the universe swoons with joy and rapture to look upon your glory. You are eternity, being, nonbeing and beyond." *(Pause.)* And Krishna says, "To grace you, Arjuna, I have revealed my higher self to you alone. No one before you has ever beheld this...this...brilliant, total, primal..." *(Pause. OPPENHEIMER extinguishes the lighter.)*

RABI: And which are you?

OPPENHEIMER: What?

RABI: Have you become Death, Shatterer of Worlds, or are you the prince who is privileged to see this terrible thing? I'm a little worried either way.

INFINITY'S HOUSE

OPPENHEIMER: I think we're the privileged ones.

RABI: Well, if that was all we were, I'd be happy. I think the problem is that we're all Death now as well, and it's so much more complicated for us than it is for your prince. When you get to be God too...ah, well, that's when insanity really begins, doesn't it? It's so much harder to play both parts. One gets confused.

OPPENHEIMER: I'm not confused. I'm more clear on this than I have been on anything in my life.

RABI: Then why are you so worried that you're going crazy? Why can't you sleep, why do you look like a goddamn skeleton? You can talk about this with me. You have to talk about it with someone and it might as well be me. I'm here. I'm your friend.

OPPENHEIMER: But you won't understand me. You're so determined to see this in a particular way. It's because you haven't really been around it with us.

RABI: I think that's precisely why I'm the one you should talk to about this. No one else can see past just making the damn thing explode. You and I are the only people who ever talk about the implications of the thing—at least around here. And lately you won't even talk about that.

OPPENHEIMER: You don't know the kind of pressure / I've been under—

RABI: Yes I do. I can see it. But if you let the pressure blind you now, you'll never forgive yourself later if they actually use the thing.

OPPENHEIMER *(Almost inaudible)*: Of course they'll use it.

RABI: What?

OPPENHEIMER: Of course they'll use it. I always knew they would.

RABBI: But we don't even know what this thing is yet.

OPPENHEIMER: They're going to use it. At least once. Maybe twice. Probably twice.

RABI: Why?

OPPENHEIMER: Because they can. *(Pause.)*

RABI: And what are you going to do?

OPPENHEIMER: What can I do? I make the thing and then hand it over to them, with my reservations voiced, and then, after they've done

143

with it what they were always going to do with it, we begin to use whatever influence we have, and it's a lot, on the government—

RABI: —God. I remember when you said that biology made you squeamish.

OPPENHEIMER: The planes are already loaded, for Christ's sake. They've been practicing the bombing mission over Japan for months now, that was implicit in building it, you must see that. It'll be used. Once...twice. To win the war. But then, see this is the beauty part, we can keep this from becoming the secret weapon of the military. It can be ours. They need us. We've made ourselves indispensible. If we can just sit through this one bombing - calmer minds will have to prevail once the war is over.

RABI: Sit through—?

OPPENHEIMER: An international agreement will be inevitable— *because*—here we have this international group of scientists who will be the obvious basis for such an agreement. We can completely revolutionize foreign policy. We can make an enormous difference. But only if the damn thing works.

RABI: Oh, Robert, you never got over Plato and the Philosopher King. Don't you know that you're always going to be the handmaiden of the army? International agreement? How can you think that another country could possibly take us seriously if we *use* the bomb and then propose peace? You can't be serious. And the army doesn't have to listen to us. They can do whatever they damn well like—they already have, they're no fools—they got you to make a bomb for them, didn't they? Got me to spend some of my best years developing radar for them at MIT. We aren't made for this kind or work. We should have spent our time doing what we were doing before any of this happened.

You're the one who always said that a physicist's important work is invariably done in his twenties, after that it's just following through on his first insights. These were our best years. I mean, you, you could have won the Nobel by now if you'd had these years to continue your work on cosmic rays. I don't understand you. Science and the military *don't* go together. We're observers, we're scholars, we shouldn't be given death-dealing powers. I don't want this thing on my hands.

OPPENHEIMER: But it's exactly *because* of our lack of comfort with that ideology that we should have this power, because we have respect for the intricacy and the subtlety of the universe—

RABI: —Well, you say that and then—

OPPENHEIMER: —The military gives us money, prestige, the opportunity to do good. Don't you see how this might herald a new age? It may be that we've achieved a turning point—not just for military strategy, not just for scientific theory, but for mankind.

RABI: It's just a bigger weapon. That's all. And nothing scientific has happened in years. Not since 1933, when Szilard was standing on a street corner waiting for the light to change, and he realized that a self-sustaining chain reaction might be possible—that was the turning point for physics. Since then it's been administration, engineering, technology. Not physics. Not the physics you and I fell in love with. And that's not to put you down. What you've done in Los Alamos is phenomenal, just the sheer organization is astonishing. You have shown genius in that. I give you that. But I'll tell you something. The very fact you've kept all these fine minds cooperating, exhilarated, *unquestioning* for so long—that makes me nervous. In Chicago with Szilard, even MIT, you hear much more open discussion about what this is, what we're doing. Whether it's right. Sure the pace isn't as phenomenal elsewhere. People aren't as happy. But I respect it. I mean, *think* what we're doing here. How'd you do it? How'd you keep everyone so happy?

OPPENHEIMER: We knew we were changing history and altering the course of science, of *physics*, I might add. We have been given the impression, and so we have felt that the country needed us, desperately, to save lives—and not just American lives. That's how I approached it, and that's how I still approach it. Physics? When you and I went into physics years ago, we might as well have been going into theology, it was completely esoteric. But now—we have the fate of the earth in our hands. This is our moment. How could we possibly duck this great opportunity? This is where the path turns, and it is with this monster. We can change the world with it—but first we have to win the war.

INFINITY'S HOUSE

RABI: But we don't need the thing to win the war. We've as good as won the war already. And as for saving the world, well, what comes to mind is Alfred Nobel thinking that when he invented dynamite he was going to end human warfare—I know you think that's an unfair analogy—Oh, Robert, I just—you're much more hopeful about mankind than I've ever been. It's something I love in you but I don't entirely trust. I don't think you've ever had much to do with mankind. I mean, aren't you the man who didn't know about the stock-market crash until Lawrence told you about it a full year later? And that goes for all of us, we're all at least somewhat removed from the rest of the world. But it's particularly true of your people. I heard that the average age at Los Alamos is twenty-five. And these aren't even normal *young* men. We're all boys who spent our childhoods in basements, playing with radios, fooling with chemical compounds, always smarter and younger than any of the other kids around us, never at home in a group—until now. Now we're surrounded by people just as strange and obsessive as ourselves. It's this little hothouse of hybrids in the middle of the desert. Children. And all of us fascinated with gizmos—build a bomb by using the principle of fission?—Yeah, I could do that! I could do that!—and then we go off in a corner and tinker. That's what we do best and we love doing it, get such a charge out of solving these problems that we forget what it is that we're in fact bringing about. We behave as if this is just another gizmo, and, God, by far the most incredible one yet—satisfying on so many levels. But, in fact, we've never lived in this world we talk so much about. I don't think you're very familiar with human nature, really, and I don't think you know much about mankind, Robert. Forgive me. *(Pause.)*

OPPENHEIMER: I wonder why you came.

RABI: I came because I want to see it work. I'm no different than anyone else.

OPPENHEIMER *(Dry)*: Well, isn't that ironic.

RABI: Isn't it? I think I want it to work almost as badly as you do. You once said that if it works it would reaffirm your faith in the human mind.

OPPENHEIMER: Did I?

RABI: Yes. I remember distinctly. And that's the problem, isn't it? We set ourselves these challanges that have unspeakable implications and then we have to ignore those things in order to satisfy our terrible curiosity to know.

OPPENHEIMER: I don't want to talk about it anymore.

RABI: I don't blame you.

OPPENHEIMER: I don't have as much control as you think I do.

RABI: I know. That's what bothers me. *(Pause)* I think I'll leave you now. I'm not as good a friend as I thought I was. I'm sorry. *(As HE starts to leave)* Did you ever read what Gandhi said about the <u>Bhagavad-Gita</u>? He didn't think it justified killing. He said the battle field must be interpreted less literally. I think he said it should be thought of as the human soul. After all, Krishna isn't just the Lord of Discipline, isn't he also the Preserver of the Universe? *(HE leaves.)*

OPPENHEIMER: Yes, he is.

M. BUTTERFLY
by David Henry Hwang
A Paris courtroom - 1986 - Song - Gallimard (65)

Song - A Chinese spy masquerading as a woman
Gallimard - A French diplomat

French diplomat, Rene Gallimard stands trial in Paris for his scandalous affair with Song Liling, a beautiful Chinese diva who was a spy—and a man. Gallimard's thoughts wander during the trial, and here he confronts Song in his imagination.

(Music from the "Death Scene" from Butterfly blares over the house speakers. It is the loudest thing we've heard in this play. Gallimard enters, crawling towards Song's wig and kimono.)
GALLIMARD: Butterfly? Butterfly?
(Song remains a man, in the witness box, delivering a testimony we do not hear.)
GALLIMARD *(To us)*: In my moment of greatest shame, here, in this coutroom—with that...person up there, telling the world... What strikes me especially is how shallow he is, how glib and obsequious...completely...without substance! The type that prowls around discos with a gold medallion stinking of garlic. So little like my Butterfly. Yet even in this moment my mind remains agile, flip-flopping like a man on a trampoline. Even now, my picture dissolves, and I see that...witness...talking to me.
(Song suddenly stands straight up in his witness box, and looks at Gallimard.)
SONG: Yes. You. White man.
(Song steps out of the witness box, and moves downstage towards Gallimard. Light change.)
GALLIMARD *(To Song)*: Who? Me?
SONG: Do you see any other white men?
GALLIMARD: Yes. There're white men all around. This is a French courtroom.
SONG: So you are an adventurous imperialist. Tell me, why did it take you so long? To come back to this place?

148

M. BUTTERFLY

GALLIMARD: What place?

SONG: This theatre in China. Where we met many years ago.

GALLIMARD *(To us)*: And once again, against my will, I am transported.

(Chinese opera music comes up on the speakers. Song begins to do opera moves, as he did the night they met.)

SONG: Do you remember? The night you gave your heart?

GILLIMARD: It was a long time ago.

SONG: Not long enough. A night that turned your world upside down.

GALLIMARD: Perhaps.

SONG: Oh, be honest with me. What's another bit of flattery when you've already given me twenty years' worth? It's a wonder my head hasn't swollen to the size of China.

GALLIMARD: Who's to say it hasn't?

SONG: Who's to say? And what's the shame? In pride? You think I could've pulled this off if I wasn't already full of pride when we met? No, not just pride. Arrogance. It takes arrogance, really—to believe you can will, with your eyes and your lips, the destiny of another. *(He dances)* C'mon. Admit it. You still want me. Even in slacks and a button-down collar.

GALLIMARD: I don't see what the point of—

SONG: You don't? Well maybe, Rene, just maybe—I want you.

GALLIMARD: You do?

SONG: Then again, maybe I'm just playing with you. How can you tell? *(Reprising his feminine character, he sidles up to Gallimard)* "How I wish there were even a small cafe to sit in. With men in tuxedos, and cappuccinos, and bad expatriate jazz." Now you want to kiss me, don't you?

GALLIMARD *(Pulling away)*: What makes you—?

SONG: —so sure? See? I take the words from your mouth. Then I wait for you to come and retrieve them. *(He reclines on the floor)*

GALLIMARD: Why?! Why do you treat me so cruelly?

SONG: Perhaps I *was* treating you cruelly. But now—I'm being nice. Come here, my little one.

149

M. BUTTERFLY

GALLIMARD: I'm not your little one!

SONG: My mistake. It's I who am *your* little one, right?

GALLIMARD: Yes, I—

SONG: So come get your little one. If you like. I may even let you strip me.

GALLIMARD: I mean, you were! Before...but not like this!

SONG: I was? Then perhaps I still am. If you look hard enough. *(He starts to remove his clothes)*

GALLIMARD: What—what are you doing?

SONG: Helping you to see through my act.

GALLIMARD: Stop that! I don't want to! I don't—

SONG: Oh, but you asked me to strip, remember?

GALLIMARD: What? That was years ago! And I took it back!

SONG: No. You postponed it. Postponed the inevitable. Today, the inevitable has come calling.

(From the speakers, cacophony: Butterfly mixed in with Chinese gongs.)

GALLIMARD: No! Stop! I don't want to see!

SONG: Then look away.

GALLIMARD: You're only in my mind! All this is in my mind! I order you! To stop!

SONG: To what? To strip? That's just what I'm—

GALLIMARD: No! Stop! I want you—!

SONG: You want me?

GALLIMARD: To stop!

SONG: You know something, Rene? Your mouth says no, but your eyes say yes. Turn them away. I dare you.

GALLIMARD: I don't have to! Every night, you say you're going to strip, but then I beg you and you stop!

SONG: I guess tonight is different.

GALLIMARD: Why? Why should that be?

SONG: Maybe I've become frustrated. Maybe I'm saying "Look at me, you fool!" Or maybe I'm just feeling...sexy. *(He is down to his briefs)*

GALLIMARD: Please. This is unnecessary. I know what you are.

SONG: Do you? What am I?

M. BUTTERFLY

GALLIMARD: A—a man.

SONG: You don't really believe that.

GALLIMARD: Yes I do! I knew all the time somewhere that my happiness was temporary, my love a deception. But my mind kept the knowledge at bay. To make the wait bearable.

SONG: Monsieur Gallimard—the wait is over.

(Song drops his briefs. He is naked. Sound cue out. Slowly, we and Song come to the realization that what we had thought to be Gallimard's sobbing is actually his laughter.)

GALLIMARD: Oh god! What an idiot! Of course!

SONG: Rene—what?

GALLIMARD: Look at you! You're a man! *(He bursts into laughter again)*

SONG: I fail to see what's so funny!

GALLIMARD: "You fail to see—!" I mean, you never did have much of a sense of humor, did you? I just think it's ridiculously funny that I've wasted so much time on just a man!

SONG: Wait. I'm not "just a man."

GALLIMARD: No? Isn't that what you've been trying to convince me of?

SONG: Yes, but what I mean—

GALLIMARD: And now, I finally believe you, and you tell me it's not true? I think you must have some kind of identity problem.

SONG: Will you listen to me?

GALLIMARD: Why?! I've been listening to you for twenty years. Don't I deserve a vacation?

SONG: I'm not just any man!

GALLIMARD: Then, what exactly are you?

SONG: Rene, how can you ask—? Okay, what about this?

(He picks up Butterfly's robes, starts to dance around. No music.)

GALLIMARD: Yes, that's very nice. I have to admit.

(Song holds out his arm to Gallimard.)

SONG: It's the same skin you've worshiped for years. Touch it.

GALLIMARD: Yes, it does feel the same.

SONG: Now—close your eyes.

151

M. BUTTERFLY

(Song covers Gallimard's eyes with one hand. With the other, Song draws Gallimard's hand up to his face. Gallimard, like a blind man, lets his hands run over Song's face.)

GALLIMARD: This skin, I remember. The curve of her face, the softness of her cheek, her hair against the back of my hand...

SONG: I'm your Butterfly. Under the robes, beneath everything, it was always me. Now, open your eyes and admit it—you adore me. *(He removes his hand from Gallimard's eyes)*

GALLIMARD: You, who knew every inch of my desires—how could you, of all people, have made such a mistake?

SONG: What?

GALLIMARD: You showed me your true self. When all I loved was the lie. A perfect lie, which you let fall to the ground—and now, it's old and soiled.

SONG: So—you never really loved me? Only when I was playing a part?

GALLIMARD: I'm a man who loved a woman created by a man. Everything else—simply falls short.

(Pause.)

SONG: What am I supposed to do now?

GALLIMARD: You were a fine spy, Monsieur Song, with an even finer accomplice. But now I believe you should go. Get out of my life!

SONG: Go where? Rene, you can't live without me. Not after twenty years.

GALLIMARD: I certainly can't live with you—not after twenty years of betrayal.

SONG: Don't be so stubborn! Where will you go?

GALLIMARD: I have a date...with my Butterfly.

SONG: So, throw away your pride. And come...

GALLIMARD: Get away from me! Tonight, I've finally learned to tell fantasy from reality. And, knowing the difference, I choose fantasy.

SONG: *I'm* your fantasy!

GALLIMARD: You? You're as real as hamburger. Now get out! I

have a date with my Butterfly and I don't want your body polluting the room! *(He tosses Song's suit at him)* Look at these—you dress like a pimp.

SONG: Hey! These are Armani slacks and—! *(He puts on his briefs and slacks)* Let's just say...I'm disappointed in you, Rene. In the crush of your adoration, I thought you'd become something more. More like...a woman. But no. Men. You're like the rest of them. It's all in the way we dress, and make up our faces, and bat our eyelashes. You really have so little imagination!

GALLIMARD: You, Monsieur Song? Accuse me of too little imagination? You, if anyone, should know—I am pure imagination. And in imagination I will remain. Now get out!

(Gallimard bodily removes Song from the stage, taking his kimono.)

SONG: Rene! I'll never put on those robes again! You'll be sorry!

GALLIMARD *(To Song)*: I'm already sorry! *(Looking at the kimono in his hands)* Exactly as sorry...as a Butterfly.

ONLY KIDDING!
by Jim Geoghan
Nightclub basement in Brooklyn - Present - Tom (20's) - Jerry (20's)

Tom - A comedian
Jerry - Tom's partner

Tom and Jerry are a comedy team struggling to make it big in a very competative industry. When they are offered a contract with a sleazy manager, pragmatic Tom balks and an argument ensues.

JERRY: *(After a few beats, enters from the bathroom wiping his hands on a paper towel.)* Where's Sal?
TOM: He just left. How do you feel?
JERRY: Terrific! I swear, I never felt better in my whole life. Where's the contract? You didn't give it back to Sal, did you?
TOM: No, it's right here.
JERRY: *(Takes pen and readies to sign.)* Good, good...I didn't sign it yet.
TOM: Jerry...
JERRY: *(Looking at contract.)* You didn't sign it either.
TOM: I know. I thought we should talk about it first.
JERRY: What's to talk about? We're going to do the Buddy King Show. Oh, man! We're gonna be rich, you know that? *Rich!* Tommy, I'm gonna buy you your own set of Korean twins.
TOM: Jerry...
JERRY: Uh uh uh uh... I insist.
TOM: Jerry!
JERRY: Yeah?
TOM: I think signing a management contract with Sal could be the worst mistake of our entire lives.
JERRY: I think it's the best thing that ever happened to us.
TOM: Well, at least we don't disagree by much.
JERRY: Tom, Sal's got us our shot. All we have to do is sign.
TOM: All we have to do is *not* sign...keep doing good shows, get better and better as an act. We'll get on the Buddy King Show *without*

154

getting involved with Sal.

JERRY: Aw, Sal's a pussycat. So what if he's a little mobbed up?

TOM: A "little mobbed up!" He named his first born daughter Jimmy the Weasel! It's not worth it, Jerry. You should see his contract. It's for seven years. Seven *years*, Jerry.

JERRY: Seven's my lucky number.

TOM: Sal wants thirty percent *before* an agent takes his ten. He wants to put us in lounges...*lounges!* Opening for guys who sing "Feelings" and play the accordion.

JERRY: The Buddy King Show, Tommy.

TOM: Lounges don't pay more than a thousand a week. Our take-home after taxes'll be less than three hundred each. Then you've got to pay living expenses...

JERRY: I don't want to hear this!

TOM: And you get paid in chips, man. Casino chips. Sure, you can cash them in, but it's a *long* walk through the casino to the cashier's window, and I know you, Jerry. You'd never make it past the blackjack tables.

JERRY: Oh, you know me real good, don't you? So good you can fuck up the best chance of my life. Well, you don't know *shit* about me, Kelly. You don't know the way my gut *aches* to get on the Buddy King Show. "Another young comedian, and another young comedian, and a bright and funny young comedian..." but never *us*! *Me*! Twenty million people!

TOM: Jerry...

JERRY: Shut up! I've waited for that night all of my life it seems. Because sitting out there in America in some perfectly pathetic domestic situation...sitting in their ugly, drunken fat...is every mother fuckin' sonofabitch who ever shit on me! They're all out there! Married to each other, drowning in hopelessness. Watching *me*! On televisions that aren't even paid for yet! Watching *me*!!! The ones who tormented and teased and humiliated me. The bitches who giggled behind my back! Their boyfriends who stole my lunch money! The fuckheads who called me Jew boy! You know what's going on with them now?! Their lives add up to *zip*! There's Jerry Goldstein on the Buddy King

ONLY KIDDING!

Show... Their lives add up to *less* than zip. It's Jerry Goldstein.

TOM: Boy, will *they* be sorry.

JERRY: Damn right. Wonder what they'll all do.

TOM: They'll probably kill themselves.

JERRY: I could dig that. I want to do that show, Tom.

TOM: I know. And we will someday.

JERRY: I want to do it...*now!*

TOM: The price is too high.

JERRY: Don't stand in my way.

TOM: I'm right beside you. You just can't see me.

JERRY: I want you to sign this, and I want you to sign it right now.

TOM: Who are you? Have we met? You look a lot like my partner.

JERRY: Sign this.

TOM: No way.

JERRY: Your last chance. Sign it or else.

TOM: Is being pathetic an Olympic sport yet? If it is, you should try out for the team.

JERRY: You signing?

TOM: Read my lips—no fucking way!

JERRY: Get out.

TOM: What?

JERRY: I said get out.

TOM: Get out of where?

(JERRY throws a childish tantrum and begins throwing Tom's personal articles toward the door. Tom's hat, coat, briefcase all go flying at the door.)

JERRY: Get out of *here*! My dressing room! Get out of my dressing room!

TOM: You're crazy.

JERRY: We're through. I'm sick and tired of this shit! You're holding me back! We're through! Get out of here!

TOM: What are you doing?

JERRY: *Out!!! Get outta here!!! Get...out!!!*

TOM: Stop!!!

JERRY: Do this to *me*?!! Do a thing like this to *me*?!!! Who the fuck you think you are?!! You are *no one*!!!

(TOM lunges at Jerry and pins him against the wall. JERRY loses none of his rage.)

TOM: Stop it!!!

JERRY: Get *out*!!!

TOM: Stop!!!

JERRY: *Ain't shit*!!!

TOM: Stop!!!

JERRY: *Hate your fuckin' guts*!!!

(TOM Slaps Jerry hard across the face. It stops JERRY cold.)

TOM: What are you, crazy? Who sat up with you in Atlanta when you thought you were going to die? Who? You so coked up you can't remember? You remember a hundred and five fever? Who stayed up with you for two days and nights? Was it Buddy King? Was it Sal? Who got his jaw broke in Pittsburgh? You thought it'd be funny to call some guy a "dumb fuckin' Pollack!" Turns out he was! Who got his jaw broke?!! Who was it!!! A few minutes ago you were ready to burn Sal forever! Work the city, find a new agent. Burn the old one! Now you want to burn me? Just like that? Is it that easy? Is it? Is it?!! Are you in there? Are you in there somewhere?

(TOM waits for a reply. There is none. After several beats he lets go of Jerry. JERRY gathers himself and crosses to the table where HE takes a drink and sits down. HE takes one of the pens and finds a napkin on the floor, picks it up and prepares to make notes on the napkin.)

JERRY: Okay. No problem here. I'm going to do the Buddy King Show on my own. That's what I'll do. I'm going to take all the bits I thought up...do 'em on my own. Make a list here. Write them down just like you do. "Tom's a writer...the brains of the team..." Hah! You don't write. You *type*! Make a list...all our bits. Work solo and do the bits I thought up. I'm takin' my bits, Kelly. And I'm writing new ones. Brand new bits...make a list...yeah.

TOM: You didn't forget.

JERRY: What?

TOM: On stage tonight. You didn't forget the new material?

ONLY KIDDING!

JERRY: I'll write funnier stuff than *that*.

TOM: You were scared. I saw it in your eyes, Jerry. It was time to launch into the new material on stage. You took a beat, stammered around, then jumped into the old material. The safe stuff. The stuff we've done a million times. And I said to myself, "Holy shit! He's scared..." It was all over your face, man. You had the same expression you have right now.

JERRY: I'm going to send you a color TV. Kelly. A great big one. You can watch me kill on the Buddy King Show. Alone. Without you.

TOM: Yeah, sure. You do that.

JERRY: I will.

TOM: Looks like you've got everything you need. Your paper, your pencil, yourself... *(Indicates bottle.)* Your inspiration. Oops, almost forgot. Your reason. Gotta have a reason, Jer. *(Finds the cassette recorder and brings it to the table where he sets it down in front of Jerry.)* Can't do comedy without a good, solid, realistic reason. Here. *(TOM presses the play button on the recorder. We hear the same wild audience APPLAUSE and WHISTLES we heard before. JERRY listens to the machine, expressionless. TOM surveys Jerry for a few beats, then sadly exits. The LIGHT slowly fades to black.)*

PVT. WARS
by James McLure
A VA hospital - 1970's - Silvio (20's-30's) - Woodruff (30's)

Silvio - An Italian American. Street-wise, tough, but not cruel
Woodruff Gately - A young southerner, childlike

Gately and Silvio are fellow VA hospital residents. Silvio is a
slick ladies' man who has lost his manhood in an explosion in
Vietnam. His irrepressible nature helps to keep his spirits high,
however, and here he takes it upon himself to tutor Gately, a
slow literal fellow, in the ways of romance.

SILVIO: Did you ever ask yourself the secret of incredible sexual
power over women?
GATELY: No.
SILVIO: Why the nurses can't resist me?
GATELY: The nurses hate you, Silvio.
SILVIO: Ah. That's what they would have you believe.
GATELY: They got me believin' it.
SILVIO: You wanna hear a great line for picking girls up?
GATLEY: Sure.
SILVIO: Now this works best for Catholic girls.
GATELY: OK.
SILVIO: You tell 'em you're a priest.
GATELY: A priest.
SILVIO: OK. Look, we'll set the scene. This is what they call settin'
the scene. Now you're sitting there. At the table. What can this table
be?
GATELY: A table.
SILVIO: OK. We'll make it a table. We're in a night club.
GATELY: Can it be a single's joint?
SILVIO: Gately, you been to a single joint?
GATELY: No.
SILVIO: OK, I tell you what. In settin' the scene we'll make this a
single's joint.
GATELY: *(Awed.)* Where'd you learn all this?

159

PVT. WARS

SILVIO: Once I hung around a USO group that was rehearsing. A Bob Hope thing. I tell you somethin', Gately...

GATELY: Yeah.

SILVIO: Never be afraid to mingle in the arts.

GATELY: All right.

SILVIO: OK, so we're in a single's joint. And you're a broad. Everybody's being hustled. It's a fucking meat market!

GATELY: What's a nice girl like me doing in a place like this?

SILVIO: That's it! That's it! That's what's called gettin' into character!

GATELY: Am I lonely?

SILVIO: Are you lonely? A face like that. What do you think?

GATELY: I'm lonely, huh?

SILVIO: That's right. You're like ugly Catholic girls all over the world. You're like a different breed. You sit there being ugly, ruining life for everybody else.

GATELY: Are you lonely?

SILVIO: Gately! I'm a priest! Of course I'm lonely. I'm one of the loneliest, horniest guys on the face of the earth. OK, you're sitting there by yourself. So I come in; and I'm very depressed, and I'm very mysterious. So I come in.

GATELY: Hey! Look! It's a priest!

SILVIO: What are you doing?

GATELY: I'm saying hello.

SILVIO: Gately, you don't know I'm a priest.

GATELY: But aren't you wearing a priest shirt?

SILVIO: No. I'm being casual.

GATELY: But don't you have your thing on?

SILVIO: My thing?

GATELY: The collar thing.

SILVIO: No.

GATELY: But you're being mysterious?

SILVIO: Very.

GATELY: Are you being scary?

SILVIO: Gately, I don't want to *scare* them. I'm being mysterious.

160

PVT. WARS

GATELY: Like Dracula?

SILVIO: Gately, you don't listen to me anymore, Gately. That worries me, Gately. Now, we're gonna do it again. You're sitting there by yourself. You're lonely. OK, so I come in. And I'm very depressed. So I come in and I look around. No, you don't see me yet, Gately. I see you. I come over and I say, "Pardon me, miss, is this seat taken?"

GATELY: Yes, it is.

SILVIO: What?

GATELY: Buzz off.

SILVIO: No. You don't say nothing.

GATELY: You want me to call the management?

SILVIO: That's not the way it goes.

GATELY: Male chauvinist pig.

SILVIO: Gately.

GATELY: What?

SILVIO: Don't give me such a hard time, OK?

GATELY: I just want to make it realistic.

SILVIO: OK. But you're making it too realistic. We'll do it again. So you're sitting there by yourself, lonely. I come in very depressed. So I come in. I'm looking around. I'm checking things out. You don't see me yet, Gately—I see you and I come over and I say, "Pardon me, miss, but is this seat taken?"

GATELY: Well, why not.

SILVIO: Mind if I sit down?

GATELY: Well, why not.

SILVIO: May I order you another drink?

GATELY: Well, sure.

SILVIO: Bartender. Two more of the same. Do you mind if I smoke?

GATELY: Well, why not. (Silvio takes out two cigarettes, puts them in his mouth, lights them both. He offers her one.) I don't want it.

SILVIO: Why not?

GATELY: You've slobbered all over it.

SILVIO: No, I haven't.

GATELY: You've had it in your mouth.

PVT. WARS

SILVIO: Gately, take the fuckin' cigarette. *(Gately takes the cigarette.)* I hope you won't think I'm being too personal but...what's your name?

GATELY: Woodruff Gately.

SILVIO: Woodruff?

GATELY: Woodruff.

SILVIO: I've never known a girl named Woodruff before.

GATELY: You've never known a girl like me.

SILVIO; If I seem a little nervous, it's because I don't usuallly come to this kind of place. Have you ever come to this kind of place?

GATELY: I'm a Baptist.

SILVIO: You must be very lonely.

GATELY: Why, because I'm a Baptist?

SILVIO: *(Putting his hand on Gately's leg.)* Can I tell you something very personal?

GATELY: OK, but don't get smutty.

SILVIO: I just wanted to tell you that I don't get much of a chance to meet beautiful women. You see, actually, I'm a priest.

GATELY: Well, I don't get much of a chance to meet men. You see, actually, I'm a lesbian.

SILVIO: *(Angrily.)* That's it! Forget it, Gately.

GATELY: I'm sorry.

SILVIO: No! No! Let's just forget it. I try to teach you something! Give you the benefit of my experience, my life! You know what you are? I'll tell you what you are. A fucking ingrate, that's what you are. Why'd you make her a lesbian?

GATELY: I don't know.

SILVIO: Not even a priest could pick up a lesbian. Nobody could pick up a lesbian.

GATELY: A lesbian could!

SILVIO: Who cares! That does me no good. I can't become a lesbian every time I wanna get laid.

GATELY: No.

SILVIO: You see my point.

GATELY: You could become a transvestite.

PVT. WARS

SILVIO: What?

GATELY: Wear women's clothes.

SILVIO: But I don't want to wear women's clothes.

GATELY: I know you don't.

SILVIO: I know I don't, too.

GATELY: You want to wear a kilt.

SILVIO: That's right.

GATELY: Which is *nearly* women's clothes.

SILVIO: Don't you like women? *(Pause.)* Don't you? Don't you? This is a big fuckin' waste. I'll tell you something buddy, from now on, you're on your own. And I wish you luck because at the rate you're going you may *never* get laid. *(He exits. Returns.)* Gately, I'm gonna get you laid.

GATELY: You are.

SILVIO: What kind of friend would *I* be if I didn't want *you* to get laid?

GATELY: I don't know.

SILVIO: Not much of a friend, Gately. We're gonna go out and we're not coming back till we get Gately laid.

GATELY: ...Could be a long night.

A QUIET END
by Robin Swados
Apartment in NYC - Present - Billy (20-30) - Doctor (30-50)

Billy - An AIDS patient
Doctor - A psychiatrist

Here, Billy, a young man with the AIDS virus, tells his psychiatrist about his father and the feelings of lonliness and frustration that he is experiencing.

DOCTOR: When did he die?

BILLY: *(confused, a little)* What?—Who?

DOCTOR: Your father.

BIILY: When I was 19. *(a quiet laugh)* Jeez.

DOCTOR: What?

BILLY: This is funny.

DOCTOR: What?

BILLY: Max said you would do this, eventually.

DOCTOR: What's that?

BILLY: He said you would ask me about my father.

DOCTOR: I'd like to know.

BILLY: I don't mind. I just think it's kind of funny. He said, "You can talk all you want about anything else—but sooner or later they all get down to Daddy." He's had a lot of experience with therapy.

DOCTOR: Evidently. I'd still like to know. It helps me understand you better, do you see that?

BILLY: *(genuinely, but still amused)* Oh sure, sure! It's just that I was under the impression I was the one who was supposed to be doing the understanding. *(Pause.)* I don't think he was wild about the idea of starting again.

DOCTOR: I beg your pardon?

BILLY: Max.

DOCTOR: Oh. Yes. Well, as you know, this is a purely voluntary program. Nobody's forcing him to attend. Or you.

BILLY: I know.

DOCTOR: It was suggested as a means of providing the three of you

A QUIET END

with an emotional outlet you might not otherwise have—

BILLY: I know.

DOCTOR: —and also as a means of minimizing any feelings of loneliness or isolation resulting from your move into the apartment.

BILLY: *(not hostile)* Okay, okay! *(Pause.)* For your information, I've never been *less* lonely in my life. *(Pause.)* Boy oh boy. You have this way of saying things—

DOCTOR: Hmmmn?

BILLY: You kind of remind me of Max. *(Pause. Imitating the DOCTOR)* "I think you might possibly, under certain circumstances, consider eradicating any irreversible evidence of tangible..." And on and on. You know what your problem is? Prolixity. Acute. *(HE's pleased with himself. Silence.)* Sorry.

DOCTOR: Perfectly all right. *(Pause. Gravely)* So.

BILLY: *(mocking him yet again)* So. *(back to normal)* What were we...

DOCTOR: Your father.

BILLY: Right. We didn't talk much. I liked him, though.

DOCTOR: What did he die of?

BILLY: Heart. On his mail route one morning.

DOCTOR: So it was sudden.

BILLY: Yes.

DOCTOR: Where were you at the time?

BILLY: Living in an apartment about twenty miles away. He was dead when I got to the hospital.

DOCTOR: That must have been very painful.

BILLY: Yeah. My mother was there, and my kid brothers, and my little sister. They were all crying.

DOCTOR: What about you? *(Pause. BILLY stares straight ahead.)* Did you cry?

BILLY: Not right there. Later.

DOCTOR: What happened?

BILLY: *(uncomfortable)* Well, my father was dead. It was only a couple of hours later. It was winter. *(Silence.)* This weird thing happened that night when we left the hospital. I'm driving along, and there are no lights or anything, and it's really hard to see—it was the middle of nowhere—and all of a sudden I see these two eyes staring at me right in the middle of the road. It was a dog. Crazy, wild eyes. I killed him. *(Silence.)* It was so weird. I was completely freaked out. My mother and sister were totally out of it to begin with. My father wasn't even dead an hour and there I go killing this dog. *(Silence.)* A couple of hours later, I went out to the garage and looked at the front fender. It had a big dent in it, and there were spots of blood. The snow had washed most of it away. That's when I started to cry. I just kind of broke down. I'm glad my mother and sister didn't see me.

DOCTOR: Why?

BILLY: I don't know. I'm just glad. I was supposed to be strong. They needed me to be strong.

DOCTOR: How about now?

BILLY: What about it?

DOCTOR: You need them.

BILLY: Like a hole in the head!

DOCTOR: Let them be strong for you.

BILLY: Oh, they'll be strong all right. You have no idea! *(Pause.)* They know nothing about me. That's all they need, to have me march on home, totally unannounced, with exciting news from the big city. "Everybody—sit down now. There's something we all need to talk about."

DOCTOR: What do you think they'd do?

BILLY: They'd freak right out, that's what they'd do. They'd die. First I'd die, then they'd die. I can see it now—a great big old house in Mason City filled with dead people.

DOCTOR: They don't know you're gay?

BILLY: No.

DOCTOR; Are you sure?

BILLY: Oh, I am sure. *Very* sure.

DOCTOR: Are you planning on keeping it from them forever?

BILLY: Most likely, and then some. *(Silence.)* I know you think I'm doing some terrible...*injustice* to myself, to say nothing of them, by keeping it all hush-hush. You're wrong. Certain things are better left unsaid. *(Pause.)* My mother gets up every Sunday morning and goes to church. When they all sit down to dinner, someone *always* says grace. I'll bet you thought no one said grace any more. I can't just walk in there and wipe all that out.

DOCTOR: Do you think—

BILLY: I really don't wish to discuss it. Believe me, I know what it would do. It's not worth it. At some point they're going to know what happened—when I'm not around—and that'll be bad enough.

DOCTOR: Did you ever stop to think it might be worse that way?

BILLY: For them or for me?

DOCTOR: For them.

BILLY: Right. Of *course* for them. *I* won't *be* here. *(Pause. Firm.)* It's as if you're asking me to go in and have this really complex discussion about—well, like I was to go in there and speak fluent French or something, and they don't even know how to say "bonjour." You see what I mean?

DOCTOR: Language can be taught, Billy. It can also be learned.

BILLY: Well, now that is truly profound, do you know that? This is not the School of Foreign Studies we are discussing here. I'm talking about my family! I will not destroy the life they have. It's bad enough I've wrecked my own.

DOCTOR: Is that how you feel?

BILLY: Who else is to blame? The one wrong choice I made? He's got his own set of circumstances to sort through.

DOCTOR: If you found yourself face to face with him at this moment—

BILLY: I'm not.

DOCTOR: But if you did—

BILLY: But I'm not! *(Silence.)*

DOCTOR: What would you say?

BILLY: *(sighing)* I would say... *(Pause.)* I would say...I forgive you. *(Silence.)* I forgive you, and I love you.

DOCTOR: You sound as if you have a very clear picture in your head of who it is you're talking to,

BILLY: I do. *(Silence.)* I can count the number of men I slept with on one hand.

SEARCH AND DESTROY
by Howard Korder
A roadside at night - Present - Martin (30's) - Kim (30's)

Martin - A man with a vision of greatness
Kim - Martin's partner in a drug deal

Martin is determined to make it big in the motion picture industry at any cost. When his idea for a screenplay based on the life of an evangelical character is passed by, he turns with desperation to conducting a drug deal that he hopes will give him the money he needs to make his dream come alive. When the drug deal goes awry and a State Trooper is shot and killed by Kim, Martin finds himself faced with a very grim decision. Swept away by circumstances beyond his control, the mild-mannered Martin must kill Kim in order to survive.

(A field by a road. Martin with trooper's flashlight, Kim smoking ciagarette.)
KIM: Where are we?
MARTIN: I don't know.
KIM: I thought you were from New Jersey.
MARTIN: Not this part.
KIM: Sky's lit up in that direction.
MARTIN: It's a refinery. They're all up and down here. We should have stayed on the Parkway.
KIM: You might want to shut that off.
(Martin shuts off flashlight. Pause.)
MARTIN: What are we going to do.
KIM: I'm going to enjoy this cigarette.
MARTIN: Why didn't you tell me Kim.
KIM: You know I've been afraid, I'll say it now, really afraid. Afraid to be tested, it's true. Afraid I wouldn't be strong, always. But I *was*. I *was*. You *saw* that I was.
MARTIN: Kim, you should have *told* me.
KIM: What did you want to know, I was *ready*, look how this hand's shaking.

168

SEARCH AND DESTROY

MARTIN: That you had a *gun*, a fucking *gun*.

KIM: Can't have an adventure without a gun.

MARTIN: Fuck adventure this was my *business*.

KIM: Whatever you want to call it.

MARTIN: No Kim, no, my *business* we were conducting, not some, some, in the street that you read about, a guy some bracelet he gets... *shot* Jesus *Christ* there's blood on my shirt.

KIM: Would you rather be arrested?

MARTIN: I don't know.

KIM: You must have an *opinion*.

MARTIN: I DON'T KNOW. MY BRAIN'S GONE AND I CAN'T THINK ANYMORE. *(Pause.)*

KIM: Let me tell you something, Martin. It might help you, because it's true. Everything...*everything* up to this exact moment...is the Past. We're done with it. You're concerned about that policeman? I am not. It's so clear to me. What did he want to do? Take what we have and punish us. By whose authority? Not mine, Martin. Not mine. This is so *clear* now. It's a dead little planet we're standing on. I'm alive. And I don't need to be forgiven one goddamn thing. Do you? *(Pause)* Now we have several possibilities spread before us. We can go on debating ethics in the middle of a marsh. We can ease up to the next state trooper and turn ouselves in. Or we can drive back to Manhattan secure in the knowledge that we are two polite young white men in well-cut suits and will...not...be...touched. Because we set the standards. And we judge *ourselves* accordingly. *(Pause)* It's freedom, Martin. I am talking to you about being free. *(Pause.)*

MARTIN: I'm done.

KIM: What's that mean.

MARTIN: I'm finished with it.

KIM: Just like that.

MARTIN: Yes.

KIM: I thought you wanted to be a threat.

MARTIN: I don't know what I "wanted to *be*." I can't *remember*. I've eaten myself up and there's nothing left. *Nothing*.

KIM: You're very weak. Aren't you.

SEARCH AND DESTROY

MARTIN: I *am*, so fuck it. Fuck the coke. Fuck the money, fuck *all* money. And fuck the movie. I won't make it. Who was I kidding. It's shit anyway—

KIM: Is it?

MARTIN: *Yes*, let's say it, that book is just *shit*. Some fucking fantasy about power and, and, "everything is possible," where *are* they, where are these "possibilities," I don't see them, *this* is it, this is life and that's ALL IT WILL EVER BE.

KIM: Where are you going, Martin.

MARTIN: To find the highway, Let go of me.

KIM: That's a bad idea, Martin. *(Martin keeps walking.)* Martin. This is your mess.

MARTIN: Fuck it.

KIM: Your *mess*, Martin, I won't get stuck with it... *(Martin keeps walking.)* Hey. You. Little man. *(He takes out the gun and shoots. Martin shouts and falls. Kim starts toward him.)* I *bet* that hurts, huh.

MARTIN: You bastard...we're *partners*...

KIM: You just changed that didn't you. *(He reaches Martin)* Finish what you start. *(He puts the gun against Martin's head)*

MARTIN: Kim. Please.

KIM: Hmm.

MARTIN: I can't face it, I can't I can't, I'm scared, I'm so scared...

KIM: I'm sorry for you. *(He pulls the trigger. Gun jams. Pause.)* Would you give me that?

MARTIN: What?

KIM: Give me the flashlight please?

MARTIN: No...

KIM: Come on.

MARTIN: HELP ME! SOMEBODY HELP ME!

KIM: Shh. Quiet. Don't be frightened.

MARTIN: *Fuck* you...

KIM: Yes, all right. Just give me the flashlight. Come on. You know you're not up to this. Give me the flashlight everything will be okay. Nothing to get alarmed about. You're safe. You are. You really are. *(Pause.)*

SEARCH AND DESTROY

MARTIN: Here.
(He butts Kim in the face with the flashlight.   Kim staggers back. Martin clubs him again, swinging wildy.)
MARTIN: You *want* this? You *want* it? Take it, *take* it!
KIM: Martin—okay—
MARTIN: HERE'S YOUR THREAT.
KIM *(Collapsing)*: Uh—
MARTIN: HERE'S YOUR POSSIBLE. HERE'S YOUR SAFETY, YOU FEEL THAT?
(Kim stops moving. Martin keeps beating him.)
MARTIN: GET UP. GET UP. I'M READY. I AM NOT AFRAID. I AM NOT AFRAID.
(Kim lies face down. Martin lowers his arms. Long pause.)
MARTIN: Kim. Hey. Look at this. Look at it you fuck. *(He pushes Kim over with his foot and displays the flashlight barrel)* That's your blood. You see it? That's *your* blood. Here's what I know. I'm stronger than you.

SPEED-THE-PLOW
by David Mamet
Hollywood - Present - Fox (40's) - Gould (40's)

Bobby Gould - A movie producer
Charlie Fox - Gould's business associate

Charlie Fox brings his boss, Bobby Gould, a hot script that one
of Hollywood's top director's dropped on his lap. A potential
money-maker, replete with sex and violence. Karen, Gould's
temporary secretary, has an "arty" script that she wants to
promote. Fox and Gould have come to an agreement over the
script and have decided to lunch together. Gould bets Fox that
he can make a successful pass at his new secretary.

FOX: Lunch at the Coventry.
GOULD: That's right.
FOX: Thy will be done.
GOULD: You see, all that you got to do is eat my doo doo for eleven
years, and eventually the wheel comes round.
FOX: Pay back time.
GOULD: You brought me the Doug Brown script.
FOX: Glad I could do it.
GOULD: You son of a *bitch*...
FOX: Hey.
GOULD: Char, I just hope.
FOX: What?
GOULD: The shoe was on the other foot, I'd act in such a...
FOX: ...Hey...
GOULD: Really, princely way toward *you*.
FOX: I *know* you would, Bob, because lemme tell you: experiences
like this, *films* like this...these are the films...
GOULD: ...Yes...
FOX: *These* are the films that whaddayacallit... *(long pause)* That
make it all worthwhile.
GOULD: ...I think you're going to find a *lot* of things now, make it
all worthwhile. I think *conservatively*, you and me, we build ourselves

172

in to split, minimally, ten percent. *(pause)*

FOX: Of the net.

GOULD: Char, Charlie: permit me to tell you: two things I've learned, twenty five years in the entertainment industry.

FOX: What?

GOULD: The two things which are always true.

FOX: One:

GOULD: The first one is: there is no net.

FOX: Yeah...? *(pause)*

GOULD: And I forget the second one. Okay, I'm gonna meet you at the Coventry in half an hour. We'll talk about boys and clothes.

FOX: Whaddaya gonna do the interim?

GOULD: I'm gonna *work*... *(indicating his figures on the pad)*

FOX: Work...? You never did a day's work in your life.

GOULD: Oooh, oooh...the bitching lamp is lit.

FOX: You never did a fucken' day's work in your life.

GOULD: That true?

FOX: Eleven years I've know you, you're either scheming or you're ziggin' and zaggin', hey, I *know* you, Bob.

GOULD: Oh yes, the scorn of the impotent...

FOX: I know you, Bob. I know you from the *back*. I know what you're staying for.

GOULD: You do?

FOX: Yes.

GOULD: What?

FOX: You're staying to hide the afikomen.

GOULD: Yeah?

FOX: You're staying here to put those moves on your new secretary.

GOULD: I am?

FOX: Yeah, and it *will* not work.

GOULD: It will not work, what are you saying...?

FOX: No, I was just saying that she...

GOULD: ...she wouldn't go for me.

FOX: That she won't go for you.

GOULD: *(pause)* Why?

173

FOX: Why? *(pause)* *I* don't know.

GOULD: What do you see...?

FOX: I think...I think...you serious?

GOULD: Yes.

FOX: I don't want to pee on your parade.

GOULD: No.

FOX: I mean, I'm sorry that I took the edge off it.

GOULD: I wasn't *going* to hit on her.

FOX: Hmmm.

GOULD: I was gonna...

FOX: You were gonna work.

GOULD: Yes.

FOX: Oh.

GOULD: *(pause)* But tell me what you see.

FOX: What I see, what I *saw*, just an observation...

GOULD: ...Yes...

FOX: It's not important.

GOULD: Tell me what you see. Really.

FOX: I just thought, I just thought she falls between two stools.

GOULD: And what would those stools be?

FOX: That she is not, just some, you know, a "floozy"...

GOULD: A "floozy"...

FOX: ...on the other hand, I think I'd have to say, I don't think she is so *ambitious* she would schtup you just to get ahead. *(pause)* That's all. *(pause)*

GOULD: What if she just "liked" me? *(pause)*

FOX: If she just "liked" you?

GOULD: Yes.

FOX: Ummm. *(pause)*

GOULD: Yes.

FOX: You're saying, if she just...*liked* you... *(pause)*

GOULD: You mean nobody loves me for myself.

FOX: No.

GOULD: No?

FOX: Not in *this* office...

SPEED-THE-PLOW

GOULD: And she's neither, what, vacant nor ambitious enought to go...

FOX: ...I'm not saying you don't *deserve* it, you *do* deserve it. Hey...I think you're worth it.

GOULD: Thank you. You're saying that she's neither, what, dumb, nor ambitious enough, she would go to bed with me.

FOX: ...She's too, she's too...

GOULD: She's too...high-line...?

FOX: No, she's, she's too...

GOULD: She's too...

FOX: ...yes.

GOULD: Then what's she doing in this office?

FOX: She's a *temporary* worker.

GOULD: You're full of it, Chuck.

FOX: Maybe. And I didn't mean to take the *shine* off our...

GOULD: Hey, hey, he sends the cross, he sends the strength to bear it. Go to, go to lunch, I'll meet you at...

FOX: I didn't mean to imply...

GOULD: Imply. Naaa. Nobody loves me. Nobody loves me for myself. Hey, big deal, don't go mopin' on me here. We'll go and celebrate. A Douglas Brown Film. Fox and Gould...

FOX: ...you're very kind...

GOULD: ...you brought the guy in. Fox and Gould Present:

FOX: I'll see you at lunch... *(starts to Exit)*

GOULD: But I bet she would go, I bet she *would* go out with me.

FOX: I bet she would, too.

GOULD: No, no. I'm saying, I think that she "likes" me.

FOX: Yeah. I'm sure she does.

GOULD: No, joking apart, babe. My *perceptions*... Say I'm nuts, I don't *think* so—she likes me, and she'd go out with me.

FOX: How much?

GOULD: How much? Seriously...? *(pause)*

FOX: Yeah.

GOULD: ...that she would...?

FOX: Yeah. That she would *anything*. *(pause)* That she would

175

anything. *(pause)* That she would deal with you in any other than a professional way. *(pause)*

GOULD: Well, my, my, my, my, my.

FOX: What can I tell you, "*Bob*".

GOULD: That I can get her on a date, that I can get her to my house, that I can screw her.

FOX: I don't think so.

GOULD: How much? *(pause)*

FOX: A hundred bucks.

GOULD: That's enough?

FOX: Five hundred bucks that you can't.

GOULD: Five hundred? That's enough?

FOX: A gentlemen's bet.

GOULD: Done. Now get out of here, and let me work...the Coventry at one. I need...

FOX: The script, the budget, chain of ownership...

GOULD: Good.

FOX: I'll swing by my, I'll bring it to lunch.

GOULD: Good. Char... *(pause)*

FOX: What?

GOULD: Thank you.

FOX: Hey. Fuck you.

SPOILS OF WAR
by Michael Weller
Greenwich Village - 1950's - Andrew (40's) - Martin (16)

Andrew - An estranged father
Martin - Andrew's son

Father and son have recently been reunited after several years of separation. When Martin visits his father, he proves to be intent on patching up his dysfunctional family as can be seen in the following exchange.

ANDREW: Deet-deet-deet, red light, emergency...

MARTIN: *(taken by surprise)* You said a routine landing...

ANDREW: You've gone red in the air, what do you do—full throttle, get away from the ground as fast as you can, and why is that?

MARTIN: I forgot...

ANDREW: 'Cause we're soft and...

BOTH: ...the ground is hard, it's no contest!

ANDREW: Okay, I threw you a little zinger there. You did well. Naaah, you did just great. Keep it up and we might get you into a real machine this summer...

MARTIN: A DC-7?

ANDREW: Whoa! That's a big bird you're talking about. Doubt I could fly one of those myself.

MARTIN: Why not, you're a pilot.

ANDREW: *(amused)* I'm a photographer, kiddo. I happen to be shooting a spread for the airline, bummed a few free lessons for the hell of it.

MARTIN: You're going to solo round the world, that's what you said.

ANDREW: I said *maybe*, and till maybe happens, what do we call it?

MARTIN: A pipe dream.

ANDREW: There you go, now back to work...

MARTIN: But say we're flying to, I don't kow, Switzerland or something, and there's an emergency, the pilot has a heart attack, you could take over and land, right?

ANDREW: There's a copilot.

SPOILS OF WAR

MARTIN: He's epileptic.

ANDREW: I'd change airline. How 'bout less with the mouth and more with the hands. *(Both return to unpacking boxes.)*

MARTIN: Great place. Kind of big for one person.

ANDREW: *(beat)* You don't mind that Penny joined us?

MARTIN: Why should I mind.

ANDREW: I'm glad you could make it over. Thought you'd have other plans, first night home from school.

MARTIN: Mom works late. It's a real hard job, lot of overtime.

ANDREW: She doesn't mind your dropping by?

MARTIN: I told you at Parents' Day, she's glad we're seeing each other. She appreciated you coming up to school when she's so busy. She want us to spend time.

ANDREW: Sounds like she's changed.

MARTIN: She's pretty great. Talks about you all the time.

ANDREW: *(abruptly)* Open that box, I'll get us a Moxie, celebrate our first evening together, what do you say? *(Re box)* You'll find something inside—it's right on top. Had it framed.

MARTIN: *(holds up framed photo)* The cowboy? What for? Hey, this is *you*!

ANDREW: Lazy-Y Ranch.

MARTIN: You were a cowboy?

ANDREW: Well, I had a hat on my head and a horse under my butt, I guess so. And a fruit picker, sign painter, even deputy sheriff up in Idaho, you name it.

MARTIN: Mom never said.

ANDREW: Listen, kiddo. I quit school. I quit 'cause nothing made sense, what I saw going on around me—newspapers screaming prosperity, growth, record employment, while my dad and damn near everyone we knew could barely put meat on the table once a week, and still they believed the headlines. So, one day, bang, out the door, age fifteen, rode the rails west to see for myself, and you know what? After five years of knocking around, I knew the truth. The papers were lying. That's right. This country was a total god damn disaster. And they kept right on lying all the way to '29, when things got so bad they

just couldn't anymore. You hold onto that *(the photo)* and remember—
don't believe what they tell you. Go out and see for yourself. You
know why I'm saying this?

MARTIN: Aren't we just talking?

ANDREW: I never "just talk." Think about it. I was in school;
you're in school. I headed west; you're heading to Europe. Well?

MARTIN: *(puzzled)* Going away, is that what you mean?

ANDREW: I mean what's true and what's not true. I mean that essay
of yours, the one you read at school.

MARTIN: The Cold War? What about it?

ANDREW: That's what I'd like to know. What about it?

MARTIN: *(still puzzled)* It won the contest. *(brighter)* They're gonna
publish it in *Roots and Branches*, that's the yearbook, I can save you a
copy. *(He is trying to slip out of this, lifting box to carry elsewhere.)*

ANDREW: Look at me, Marty. Tell me how it went.

MARTIN: I didn't memorize it, Dad. "The Cold War is both a war
and not a war," something like that...

ANDREW: Keep going.

MARTIN: You heard it at Parent's Day.

ANDREW: Refresh my memory.

MARTIN: "It is two great powers, Russia and America, pitting their
citizens against each other with propaganda, lies and silence-"

ANDREW: To me, Marty, to *me*.

MARTIN: *(braving it)* But perhaps we have more in common than we
know. Take our very initials, U.S., and U.S.S.R., both begin with *US*,
and does this not suggest a greater unity...

ANDREW: Good, you're blushing...

MARTIN: I am not.

ANDREW: It's bullshit, and you know it. You're just parroting back
what you know they want to hear up at that circus of a school,
"International Brotherhood of Man"...Christ alive...

MARTIN: Take it easy, that's just the motto...

ANDREW: It's a wet dream for radical has-beens. They hire a staff
of academic rejects from around the world—at half price—and call it a
Global Environment. How could she get suckered in, after everything

179

we fought for back then.

MARTIN: Look, if you don't like the place, why don't you call Mom and we'll all get together and talk it over.

ANDREW: *(beat)* Knowledge is everything, Marty. Everything. I don't want to see you open your mouth ever again to please another man. You say only what you truly believe, or you shut up.

MARTIN: Dad, what if... Say I hadn't written that essay.

ANDREW: Did you?

MARTIN: Sort of. Not really. I cribbed it from this U.N. journal in the school library. I didn't mean for it to get all out of hand like this. *(beat)* Dad?

ANDREW: All right. Put it out of your head, I don't think you're that kind of kid. Are you?

MARTIN: I thought they'd catch me. I thought I'd be sent home. Someone has to be with her.

ANDREW: Who? Wait a minute. You tried to get yourself booted on her account?

MARTIN: *(agitated)* She pretends everything's okay, but I know she doesn't mean it, not this time, or maybe it's just different now 'cause it was always, before, when we moved someplace she'd make it a big adventure and it was all going to be fine, but nothing's working out the way she planned and I don't know how to make it better—she doesn't eat right, she gives her money away, she forgets to pay her bills and now I'll be gone all year—

ANDREW: Stop right there. That woman is tough as old leather, and always has been. She doesn't want help. People have tried, believe me. You carry your own load, Martin. She'll be fine. Do you understand me.

MARTIN: Yes, sir.

ANDREW: Now let's have that Moxie.

TEMPTATION
by Vaclav Havel
translated by Marie Winn
A scientific institute - Present - Foustka (30-40) - Fistula (50+)

Foustka - A scientist tempted by a mysterious stranger to dabble
    with witchcraft
Fistula - A wily old cripple who may or may not be the Devil

Foustka is a modern version of Dr. Faust; a man of science
tempted by the mysterious Fistula to indulge in the forbidden
practice of witchcraft. Here, the cunning Fistula offers to make
Foustka's secretary fall in love with him as proof of his powers.

FOUSTKA: Good evening.
FISTULA: Greetings. *(Pause. Looks around him with interest)* What
a cozy place you have here, just as I'd imagined it. Good books—a
rare globe—everything somehow as it ought to be—the balances don't
lie.
FOUSTKA: I don't know what balances you're talking about. But first
of all I don't even know who I'm speaking to...
FISTULA: All in good time. May I sit down?
FOUSTKA: Please.
*(Fistula sits on the couch. Takes off his shoes, removes the slippers
from the paper bag, puts them on, puts the shoes into the bag, and then
places it on the sofa beside him. A pause.)*
FISTULA: I assume that I don't have to ask you not to mention my
visit to anyone, for your sake as well as mine.
FOUSTKA: Why shouldn't I mention it?
FISTULA: You'll see why soon enough. My name is Fistula. Where
I'm employed is no importance, and in any event I don't even have a
permanent position, nor do I need to have one, since I'm a cripple with
a pension. *(Grins stupidly as if he has made a joke)*
FOUSTKA: I'd guess that you work for a safety-match factory.
FISTULA *(Chuckles, then suddenly grows serious)*: That comes from
a certain unidentified fungus of the foot. It makes me quite miserable
and I do what I can for it, even though there's not much I can do.

TEMPTATION

(Foustka sits on the corner of the desk and looks at Fistula. In his look we sense a mixture of curiosity, mistrust, and revulsion. A longer pause.)

FISTULA: Aren't you going to ask me what I want or why I've come?

FOUSTKA: I'm ever hopeful that you'll tell me that yourself.

FISTULA: That, of course, would be quite possible, but I had a particular reason for not doing it until now.

FOUSTKA: What was it?

FISTULA: I was interested to see whether you'd figure it out for yourself.

FOUSTKA *(Irately)*: How could I figure it out when I've never seen you before in my life! In any case, I have neither the time nor the inclination to play guessing games with you. Unlike you, I happen to have a job and I'm leaving in a few minutes...

FISTULA: For the office party, right? But you've got heaps of time for that!

FOUSTKA: How do you know that I'm going to the office party?

FISTULA: And before my arrival you weren't exactly behaving like someone in a hurry either...

FOUSTKA: You don't know a thing about what I was doing before your arrival.

FISTULA: I beg your pardon, but I certainly know better than you do what I know and what I don't know, and how I know what I know!

(Fistula grins stupidly. A longer pause. Then Foustka stand up, crosses to the other side of his desk, and turns gravely to Fistula.)

FOUSTKA: Look, Mister...

FISTULA: Fistula.

FOUSTKA: Look, Mister Fistula, I'm asking you plainly and simply, in all seriousness, and I'm expecting a plain and simple, serious answer from you: What do you want?

(A short pause.)

FISTULA: Does the name Marbuel say anything to you? Or Loradiel? Or Lafiel?

(Foustka gives a start, quickly regains his control, gives a long shocked look at Fistula.)

182

TEMPTATION

FOUSTKA *(Exclaiming)*: Out!

FISTULA: Excuse me?

FOUSTKA: I said: Out!

FISTULA: What do you mean—out?

FOUSTKA: Leave my apartment immediately and never set foot in it again!

(Fistula rubs his hands contentedly.)

FOUSTKA: Did you hear me?

FISTULA: I heard you clearly and I'm delighted by this reaction of yours because it absolutely confirms that I've come to the right place.

FOUSTKA: What do you mean?

FISTULA: Your fright, don't you see, makes it perfectly clear that you're fully aware of the importance of my contacts, which you wouldn't be if you hadn't been interested in the aforementioned powers earlier.

FOUSTKA: Those names don't mean a thing to me, I haven't the faintest idea of what you're talking about; moreover, the suddenness of my demand that you leave merely reflected the suddenness with which I became fed up with you. My disgust coming at the same time that you pronounced those names was a complete coincidence! And now, having given you this explanation, I can only repeat what I said before, but this time without any fear that you might mistake my meaning: Leave my apartment immediately and never set foot in it again!

FISTULA: Your first request for me to leave—that I'll naturally grant, though probably not quite immediately. Your second request I will not grant, for which you will be very grateful to me later on.

FOUSTKA: You missed my meaning. Those weren't two independent requests, in fact they weren't request at all. It was a demand—a single and indivisible one at that!

FISTULA: I'll make a note of it. But I'd also like to point something out: the haste with which you slipped in an additional motivation for your demand, together with the interesting fact that even though you claimed to be fed up with me, you considered it important enough to slip in this additional motivation even at the risk of delaying my longed-for departure—that haste together with that interesting fact are proof to

183

me of one single thing: that your orginal fear of me as a middleman for certain contacts has now been superseded by a fear of me as a potential informer. Let me assure you, however, that I was counting on this phase as well. In fact had it not set in I would have felt quite uneasy. I would have considered it peculiar and would have wondered myself whether in fact *you* weren't an informer yourself. But now let me get down to business. There's obviously no way I can prove to you that I'm not an informer; even if I were to conjure up Ariel himself at this moment it still wouldn't eliminate the possibility of my being an informer. Therefore, you have only three choices. First, to consider me an informer and to continue to insist on my immediate departure. Second, not to consider me an informer and to trust me. Third, not to make up your mind for the time being as to whether I'm an informer or not, but to adopt a waiting attitude, meaning on the one hand not to kick me out immediately and on the other hand not to say anything in front of me that might eventually be used against you if I actually *were* an informer. I'd like to recommend the third alternative.

(Foustka paces the room deep in thought; finally he sits down at his desk and looks over at Fistula.)

FOUSTKA: Very well, I'll accept that, but I'd like to point out that there's obviously no need for me to control or restrict my speech in any way because there's absolutely nothing I could possibly think, much less say, that might possibly be used against me.

FISTULA *(Exclaiming)*: Marvelous! *(Claps his hands with pleasure)* You delight me! If I were an informer I'd have to admit that you avoided the first trap beautifully! Your declaration is clear evidence of your absolutely solid caution, intelligence, and quick wit, qualities that I eagerly welcome, since they give me hope that I'll be able to depend on you and that we'll be able to work together well.

FOUSTKA: Listen, Mister...

FISTULA: Fistula.

FOUSTKA: Listen, Mister Fistula, I'd like to tell you two things. First of all, your talk is a bit redundant for my taste. You really ought to get to the point of what brought you here more quickly. You've said virtually nothing, even though I asked you ages ago for a serious, direct, and concise answer to the question of what you actually want. And secondly, it surprises me greatly to hear that we're supposed to be working together on something. That requires two people after all...

FISTULA: Your answer had eighty-six words. Considering its semantic value that isn't exactly a small number, and if I were you I wouldn't reproach anybody too severely for redundancy.

FOUSTKA: Bullshit is infectious, as we know.

FISTULA: I hope that as time goes by you'll adopt some of my more important skills as well.

FOUSTKA: You actually want to teach me something?

FISTULA: Not only teach...

FOUSTKA: What else, for God's sake?

FISTULA *(Crying out)*: Leave him out of this!

FOUSTKA: Well, what else are you planning to do with me?

FISTULA *(Smiling)*: To initiate you...

(Foustka stands up abruptly and bangs his fist on the table.)

FOUSTKA *(Shouting)*: That's enough! I'm a scientist with a scientific outlook on life, holding down a responsible job at one of our foremost scientific establishments! If anyone were to speak in my presence in a way that's obviously intended to spread superstition, I'd be forced to proceed in accordance with my scientific conscience!

(For a moment Fistula stares stupidly at Foustka, then he suddenly begins to laugh wildly and dance around the room. Just as suddenly he falls silent, comes to a stop, stoops to the ground, and with his finger slowly traces the circle that Foustka had drawn there earlier, after which he jumps up and begins to laugh wildly again. Then he goes over to the desk, seizes one of the hidden candlesticks, waves it in the air and, still laughing, places it on the desk. Foustka watches him, goggle-eyed. Then suddenly Fistula becomes serious again, returns to the couch, and sits down.)

FISTULA *(Matter-of-factly)*: I know your views well, Doctor Foustka. I know how much you love your work at the Institute, and I apologize for my foolish joke. Anyhow, it's high time for me to cut out all this preliminary joking around. As your director emphasized again this morning, one of your Institute's tasks is to fight against certain manifestations of irrational mysticism that keep cropping up here and there as a sort of obscurely preserved residue of the prescientific thinking of primitive tribes and the Dark Ages of history. As a scientist you know perfectly well that the more thoroughly you're armed with knowledge about what you're supposed to be fighting against, that much more effective your fight will be. You have at your disposal quite a decent collection of occult literature—almost all the basics are here, from Agrippa and Nostradamus to Eliphas Levy and Papus-nevertheless, theory isn't everything, and I can't believe that you've never felt the need to acquaint yourself with the practice of black magic directly. I come to you as a sorcerer with several hundred successful magical and theurgical evocations under his belt who is ready and willing to acquaint you with certain aspects of this practice in order to give you a base for your scientific studies. And in case you're asking yourself why in the world a sorcerer should want to join a battle against witchcraft, I can even give you a convincing reply to that: I seem to be in a tricky situation in which I might come to a bad end without cover of some sort. I am therefore offering you my own self for study, and I ask nothing in return besides your vouching for me, if the need arises, that I turned myself over to the disposition of science, and that therefore it would be unfair to hold me responsible for the propagation of something which, in reality, I was helping to fight against.

(Fistula looks gravely at Foustka; Foustka reflects.)

FOUSTKA *(Quietly)*: I have a suggestion.

FISTULA: I'm listening.

FOUSTKA: To expedite our communications I'm going to pretend that I'm not endowed with a scientific outlook and that I'm interested in certain things purely out of curiosity.

FISTULA: I accept your suggestion!

(Fistula steps up to Foustka and offers him his hand; Foustka hesitates a moment, then gives his hand to Fistula, who clasps it. Foustka intantly pulls his hand away in alarm.)

FOUSTKA *(Crying out)*: Ow! *(Gasps with pain, rubs his hand and waves it in th air)* Man, your temperature must be fifty below zero.

FISTULA *(Laughing)*: Not quite.

TEMPTATION

(Foustka finally recovers and resumes his seat at his desk.   Fistula also sits down, folds his hands in his lap, and stares with theartically doglike resignation at Foustka.   A long pause.)

FOUSTKA: So?

(A long pause.)

FOUSTKA: What's going on?

(A long pause.)

FOUSTKA: What's wrong with you.   Have you lost your tongue all of a sudden?

FISTULA: I'm waiting.

FOUSTKA: For what?

FISTULA: For your command.

FOUSTKA: I don't understand: What command?

FISTULA: What better way for me to acquaint you with my work than for you to assign me certain tasks whose fulfillment you can verify for yourself and whose fulfillment matters to you for some reason?

FOUSTKA: Aha, I see.   And what kind of tasks—roughly—should they be?

FISTULA: That's for you to say!

FOUSTKA: All right—but still and all—it's hard to think of anything under the circumstances...

FISTULA: Don't worry, I'll help you out.   I think I have an idea for an innocent little beginning of sorts.   If I'm not mistaken, there's a certain young lady you admire.

FOUSTKA: I don't know what you're talking about.

FISTULA: Doctor Foustka, after everything we've said here, you really must admit that I might occasionally know somebody's little secret.

FOUSTKA: If you're talking about the secretary of our Institute, I'm not denying that she's a pretty girl, but that doesn't necessarily mean...

FISTULA: What if tonight at the office party—quite unexpectedly and of course quite briefly—she were to fall in love with you?   How about that?

(Foustka paces nervously for a short while, and then turns abruptly to Fistula.)

FOUSTKA: Please leave!

187

TEMPTATION

FISTULA: Me? Why?

FOUSTKA: I repeat—go away!

FISTULA: Are you beginning that again? I thought we'd reached an agreement.

FOUSTKA: You've insulted me.

FISTULA: How? In what way?

FOUSTKA: I'm not so badly off as to need magic for help in my love life! I'm neither a weakling incapable of manfully facing the facts when he doesn't manage to win by his own efforts, nor a cad who would carry out experiments on innocent and completely unsuspecting young girls for his own sensual pleasure. Do you take me for some kind of Bluebeard or what, Fistula?

FISTULA: Which of us knows what we really are! But that's not the issue now. If my well-intentioned, innocent, and quite spur-of-the-moment little idea touched a raw nerve for some reason, I naturally apologize and withdraw it!

FOUSTKA: And I didn't even mention my main objection: I'm involved in a serious relationship, and I'm faithful to my girlfriend.

FISTULA: Just as faithful as she is to you?

FOUSTKA *(Startled)*: What do you mean by that?

FISTULA: Forget it.

FOUSTKA: Wait a minute, I'm not going to let you get away with making dirty insinuations like that! I'm not interested in gossip, and I don't like impudence!

FISTULA: I'm sorry I said anything. If you've decided to be blind, that's your business.

(Fistula removes his shoes from his paper bag and slowly begins to change footgear. Foustka watches him uneasily. A pause.)

FOUSTKA: You're leaving? *(Pause)* I guess I blew up a little.

(Pause. Fistula has changed into his shoes, places his slippers in the bag, stands up, and slowly walks towards the door.)

FOUSTKA: So what's going to happen?

FISTULA *(Stops and turns around)*: With what?

FOUSTKA: Well, with our agreement.

FISTULA: What about it?

FOUSTKA: Is it on?

FISTULA: That depends entirely on you. *(He grins)*

THE TRAVELLING SQUIRREL
by Robert Lord
Manhattan - Present - Bart (20's-30's) - Wally (30's-40's)

Bart - A struggling writer
Wally - A flamboyant gossip columnist

Bart is struggling as a writer, working as a typesetter to support himself. His wife, Jane, is a successful soap opera actress. Here, Bart banters with Wally, a gossip columnist he has just met at a party.

WALLY: How do you do? I'm Wallace White, the host. Who are you? When did we meet? We have met, haven't we? We must've. It stands to reason. If we hadn't met, we wouldn't know each other, would we? You wouldn't be here. Don't you love logic? It's so ruthless. I hope you're not a gate-crasher. I didn't catch your name.
BART: Bart.
WALLY: Bart? Just Bart? You only have one name? Like Madonna? Fabian? Capucine?
BART: Bart Babbington.
WALLY: Of the Babbington Babbingtons? How wonderful! I adore Maine. All those churches. It's so Episcopalian. I've been to the Bar Harbor house. Divine. And Lally, Lally Babbington, what a gem. She must be your aunt.
BART: As a matter of fact...
WALLY: She couldn't possibly be your mother?
BART: We're not related.
WALLY: You're a New Hampshire Babbington? Quell embarrassment. We're talking Hatfields and McCoys. Lally clued me in. Not that I have any feelings one way or the other. I'm perfectly impartial. You're the first New Hampshire Babbington I've ever met.
BART: I've never been to New Hampshire.
WALLY: What went on? Long distance conception?
BART: I'm from New Jersey.
WALLY: New Jersey?
BART: Secaucus.

THE TRAVELLING SQUIRELL

WALLY: I don't know any Secaucus Babbingtons.

BART: That's not surprising. It was all a mistake. Our Winnebago was forced off the interstate by a drunk driver who had it in for circus people.

WALLY: Circus people?

BART: His daughter was inadvertantly impregnated by a lion tamer with the Ringling Brothers. I was born on a grassy knoll overlooking the Walt Whitman comfort station.

WALLY: What are you talking about?

BART: My father swallowed swords. It runs in the family. Do you have any gladioli?

WALLY: What on earth for?

BART: They're so much safer than swords.

A WALK IN THE WOODS
by Lee Blessing
A woods outside Geneva - Botvinnik (57) - Honeyman (45)

Botvinnik - A canny Russian diplomat
Honeyman - A determined American diplomat

John Honeyman has been assigned to negotiate arms treaties with
Andrey Botvinnik, his Soviet counterpart in Geneva.   Crafty
Botvinnik has been playing the diplomacy game for a long time,
and encourages the straight-laced Honeyman to deviate from
protocol by going for a walk in the woods.

BOTVINNIK: Your home city.   What is it—Wausau?   *(This he
pronounces poorly—something like: Vah-sow.)*
HONEYMAN: Wausau.
BOTVINNIK: *(Nodding, as though their pronunciations match.)* Vah-
sow.
HONEYMAN: No. No, Wau-sau. Wausau, Winconsin. Andrey, if
I was harsh, it's only because...
BOTVINNIK: *(Practicing it, but no better.)* Vah-sow.
HONEYMAN: Andrey...
BOTVINNIK: I think I have it now: Vah-sow.
HONEYMAN: *(Angrily.)* Wausau! It's Wausau! You can say it, you
speak English perfectly!
BOTVINNIK: I'm only trying to...
HONEYMAN: You're only trying to irritate me! I can see that! But
why!? Do you feel it gives you the upper hand? It doesn't. If these
talks fail, we both look bad. You realize that, don't you?
BOTVINNIK: I have failed before.
HONEYMAN: I haven't. *(A beat.)* What about this tiny point?
When can we expect movement from you side?
BOTVINNIK: After your election.
HONEYMAN: That's five weeks from now.
BOTVINNIK: We can only go so fast. We have hawks and doves,
just like you. Sometimes the hawks eat a few doves.
HONEYMAN: This is ludicrous. The President won't accept this.

A WALK IN THE WOODS

BOTVINNIK: He'll have no choice.

HONEYMAN: What if we force the matter?

BOTVINNIK: You could lose the whole proposal.

HONEYMAN: Of course you have to say that.

BOTVINNIK: *(With a tone of complete frankness.)* You'll lose the proposal. *(Honeyman walks away from Botvinnik, kicks at the ground angrily.)* A frustrating business, yes?

HONEYMAN: Quiet please.

BOTVINNIK: You're upset. Perhaps you would like to be alone. I can go back now. Excuse me. *(Botvinnik starts out.)*

HONEYMAN: Andrey.

BOTVINNIK: Yes?

HONEYMAN: If we go back so soon the reporters might think we're in trouble on this.

BOTVINNIK: We are in trouble on this.

HONEYMAN: There's no reason for *them* to think so.

BOTVINNIK: I thought you believed in freedom of the press.

HONEYMAN: Don't be cute. Come back and sit down.

BOTVINNIK: *(Returning to the bench.)* What shall we talk about?

HONEYMAN: We don't have to talk about anything. We just have to wait here a decent amount of time.

BOTVINNIK: Ah. *(Honeyman sits beside him. The two men stare out in different directions for a long moment.)* How are we doing?

HONEYMAN: You could use your influence, you know. They listen to you about these things.

BOTVINNIK: Not always.

HONEYMAN: Sometimes. So why not talk to them?

BOTVINNIK: It can be risky. It could put me out of fashion with the leadership.

HONEYMAN: Out of fashion?

BOTVINNIK: It's not an insignificant risk. *(A beat.)*

HONEYMAN: Could anything induce you to take that risk?

BOTVINNIK: *(His face lighting up expectantly.)* Is this a bribe?

HONEYMAN: No.

BOTVINNIK: Too bad. I never accept bribes, but I love to know what's being offered.

HONEYMAN: I mean, is there anything we can do to convince you to help? That's all I mean.

BOTVINNIK: What can the Americans do? To make me want to take chances with my career?

HONEYMAN: Yes.

BOTVINNIK: Absolutely nothing. *(Honeyman gives a short sigh of frustration.)* Now ask me what you can do.

HONEYMAN: You just said. We can't...

BOTVINNIK: No, no—you. John Honeyman. What can you do to get me to help. Ask me that. *(Honeyman eyes him distrustfully.)*

HONEYMAN: What...um, what is there I can do?

BOTVINNIK: Are you sure you want to know?

HONEYMAN: Yes, I want to know.

BOTVINNIK: Are you completely sure?

HONEYMAN: Tell me. What can I do?

BOTVINNIK: *(Almost conspiratorial.)* Be frivolous with me.

HONEYMAN: Frivolous?

BOTVINNIK: Yes. Frivolous. *(A beat.)*

HONEYMAN: What does...frivolous mean?

BOTVINNIK: It's your language.

HONEYMAN: I know.

BOTVINNIK: Don't you know the word?

HONEYMAN: Of course I know the word. It's just that...

BOTVINNIK: *(Finishing his sentence for him.)* A word may have many meanings.

HONEYMAN: Exactly.

BOTVINNIK: What do you think I mean? By frivolous. Do you think I mean playful? Impractical? *(Honeyman stares at him cautiously.)* Irrelevant? Unimportant? Superficial? *(A beat.)* With unbecoming levity? *(Honeyman rises, moves off a step or two.)* I am sorry. To me, frivolous means not serious.

HONEYMAN: Not serious? That's all? Just...not serious?

BOTVINNIK: That's all.

HONEYMAN: You want to have a...frivolous conversation?

193

(Botvinnik smiles.) And for that you'd be willing to try and influence your superiors? If I gave you that? *(Botvinnik nods.)* Why?

BOTVINNIK: Nothing else is interesting to me. Whenever I speak with Americans, they always ask. "What about war? What about Afghanistan? What about cruise missiles?" It is no longer interesting to me.

HONEYMAN: But what about cruise missiles? *(Botvinnik instantly holds up a hand in a silencing gesture.)* Sorry.

BOTVINNIK: I hear certain words—whether I say them or someone else says them—words like "detente," "human rights," "Star Wars," "Central America," "readiness," "early warning," and I feel like I am falling away from the Earth. I can see the Earth—the entire planet, like I am a cosmonaut. And it is falling away from me. We are both simply...receding into the dark. Sometimes I spend entire conversations in this kind of darkness, while I am hearing words like "summit," "test ban," "emigration," "strategic objectives." It is almost as though the words are printed...on the dark walls...all around me. And the Earth is by then like a...fingertip, it is so far away. *(A beat.)* Does this ever happen to you?

HONEYMAN: No.

BOTVINNIK: Perhaps it will someday. In any case, you must forgive me. This does not happen at the table. There, I listen very carefully. There, I pretend we are discussing a different planet from Earth, and that helps very much.

HONEYMAN: Andrey...

BOTVINNIK: Receptions, dinner parties—that's where it happens. I hear all those serious words: "lasers," "megadeaths," "acceptable losses"... Do you know what I am dying to hear an American talk about? Mickey Mouse. Cowboys. How to make a banjo...

HONEYMAN: I don't think...

BOTVINNIK: Minnie Mouse. Anything that is not serious.

HONEYMAN: I can't talk about Minnie Mouse with you.

BOTVINNIK: But that is my price. For helping you. For doing what I can.

HONEYMAN: You want to be frivolous.

A WALK IN THE WOODS

BOTVINNIK: Very much. *(A beat.)*

HONEYMAN: I'm disappointed by this. I thought you were more professional.

BOTVINNIK: This *is* professional. This is how to survive as a professional.

HONEYMAN: *(Regards him skeptically, then with resolve.)* Fine. Let's survive then. Frivolously. What shall we talk about?

BOTVINNIK: Whatever you like.

HONEYMAN: You decide; it's your idea.

BOTVINNIK: Very well, let me see. Do you like Country and Western music?

HONEYMAN: Honestly?

BOTVINNIK: Of course honestly. Why hide anything? We're being frivolous.

HONEYMAN: Yes, I do like it.

BOTVINNIK: Wonderful! So do I. It's very anti-Soviet, but nothing is perfect. *(A beat.)* *Blue Eyes Crying In the Rain*, eh?

HONEYMAN: Yes.

BOTVINNIK: Wonderful song. Very sad. It could have been Russian.

HONEYMAN: Maybe.

BOTVINNIK: Have you ever slept with a redhead?

HONEYMAN: No.

BOTVINNIK: Neither have I. It is a great regret. *(A beat. They stare out.)* You say something.

HONEYMAN: Me?

BOTVINNIK: Yes.

HONEYMAN: What should I say?

BOTVINNIK: Anything. Whatever is on your mind.

HONEYMAN: Right. Well, um...sometimes I notice when we're discussing space weapons technology...

BOTVINNIK: *No!* No, no, no, no, no!

HONEYMAN: I only meant *when* we're discussing space weapons...

BOTVINNIK: No! You are too serious.

HONEYMAN: Even to mention it? On the way to something else?

A WALK IN THE WOODS

BOTVINNIK: *Too serious!* *(A beat. Botvinnik's look is fierce.)*
HONEYMAN: I'm sorry.
BOTVINNIK: No problem. Try again. Be trivial.
HONEYMAN: Well...let's see. OK, um—I hate brown suits.
BOTVINNIK: And?
HONEYMAN: And what?
BOTVINNIK: You hate brown suits, and...?
HONEYMAN: And nothing. I hate brown suits—that's all. *(Botvinnik is disappointed. He rises, walks away towards the edge of the trees.)* What's wrong? Isn't that trivial enough?
BOTVINNIK: There's a difference between trivial and boring.
HONEYMAN: That's not boring.
BOTVINNIK: Of course it is. *(Mimicking Honeyman.)* "I hate brown suits..."?
HONEYMAN: It's no more boring than your liking Willie Nelson.
BOTVINNIK: It is.
HONEYMAN: It is not.
BOTVINNIK: You are just not good at this. Admit it.
HONEYMAN: I can be as trivial as the next person. You never said I had to be trivial and entertaining at the same time.
BOTVINNIK: It goes without saying.
HONEYMAN: It does not.
BOTVINNIK: Now you are just arguing with me.
HONEYMAN: I'm not arguing.
BOTVINNIK: You are.
HONEYMAN: *Kindly stop telling me what I am and am not doing!* *(Botvinnik is delighted.)*
BOTVINNIK: That was very good. Tell me another trivial thing.
HONEYMAN: I can't.
BOTVINNIK: Of course you can. You must, if we are to have any fun.
HONEYMAN: *I* am not having fun.
BOTVINNIK: Be patient. If you stay here long enough, the only thing you'll be able to enjoy is a totally meaningless conversation.
HONEYMAN: Have you failed that much here? *(A beat.)* I'm sorry.

A WALK IN THE WOODS

I can't be frivolous anymore.

BOTVINNIK: *(Throws his hands up in mock despair.)* What can I do? He refuses to humor me. Such a small price, and he will not pay it. I'm beginning to miss Mr. McIntyre. *(Botvinnik takes out his eyedrops.)*

HONEYMAN: All I know is, considering who we are, and where we are, and what we have been sent here to do, it is literally wasting the world's time for us to be anything but deadly serious with each other.

BOTVINNIK: Wasting the world's time. I like that.

HONEYMAN: Don't grade my phrasemaking, talk to me.

BOTVINNIK: Seriously?

HONEYMAN: Seriously.

BOTVINNIK: *(Considering this, then shaking his head.)* Too boring.

HONEYMAN: *(As Botvinnik starts to put the eyedrops away.)* You know, it's a shame those tears of yours can't be real.

BOTVINNIK: *(Dropping the bottle back into his pocket.)* What if I talk seriously to you, and you don't enjoy it?

HONEYMAN: If it's serious, I'll enjoy it.

BOTVINNIK: You will, eh?

HONEYMAN: Yes.

BOTVINNIK: Very well then. *(With a sudden formality.)* I will now present to you my serious thoughts on the subject of...let's see...the character of the Russian and American people.

HONEYMAN: I don't think that's...

BOTVINNIK: That's my topic. It is fundamental. Do you object?

HONEYMAN: Not as long as you're serious.

BOTVINNIK: Deadly. *(A beat. Honeyman nods.)* Good. There is a great difference between Russians and Americans—yes or no?

HONEYMAN: Well...yes, if you...

BOTVINNIK: There is no difference. I will prove it. If the Russians and not the English had come to America, what would they have done?

HOENYMAN: They would have...

BOTVINNIK: They would have killed all the Indians and taken all the land. See? No difference. Americans and Russians are just the same. But their history is different. What is history? History is geography

197

over time. The geography of America is oceans—therefore no nearby enemies. The geography of Russia is the opposite: flat, broad plains—open invitations to anyone who wants to attack. Mongols, French, Germans, Poles, Turks, Swedes—anyone. Do you agree with this? Of course you do—it is obviously true.

HONEYMAN: Andrey...

BOTVINNIK: Quiet, I am being serious. So, what is the history of America? Conquest without competition. What is the history of Russia? Conquest *because* of competition. How best to be America? Make individual freedom your god. This allows you to attack on many fronts—all along your borders, in fact—and maintain the illusion that you are not attacking at all. You don't even have to call your wars wars. You call them "settling the west."

HONEYMAN: That's a gross misreading of...

BOTVINNIK: Don't interrupt. How best to be Russia then? Fight collectively. *Know* that you are trying to crush those around you. Make control your god, and channel the many wills of the people into one will. Only this will be effective. Only this will defeat your neighbors.

HONEYMAN: I'm leaving now.

BOTVINNIK: You can't. This is what you wanted.

HONEYMAN: I wanted a *conversation.*

BOTVINNIK: *(Pushing on.)* So—what is the result of all this history and geography? Why are the Russians and Americans—people who have done the same thing: create and maintain empires—why are we now enemies to the death?

HONEYMAN: We're not enemies, we're rival...

BOTVINNIK: We are enemies! *(A beat. Then softer.)* Because Americans, who never had to confront themselves as a conquerors, are still under the delusion that they are idealists. And Russians, who did have to confront themselves, are under the equally powerful delusion that they are realists. I'm speaking now of those in power. Common Americans and common Russians share a much simpler delusion: that they are peace-loving people.

HONEYMAN: This is profoundly cynical.

A WALK IN THE WOODS

BOTVINNIK: Thank you. I like to be clear-eyed. *(Quietly.)* You cannot work at this job as long as I have without realizing that no one wants you to succeed. Not even the man on the street.

HONEYMAN: How on earth can you think that?

BOTVINNIK: Go to the street. Ask the man. Ask him, "Do you want to get rid of all nuclear weapons right now?" Of course, he will say yes. Then ask "Are you willing to give up your country's power, prestige and predominance in the world?" He will say no. But the two questions are the same. Without nuclear weapons, our empires would no longer *be* empires. They would simply be countries among other countries.

HONEYMAN: Powerful countries.

BOTVINNIK: But not *super*powers. We are too used to dominating, John. We will never give that up.

HONEYMAN: There are other ways to be superpowers.

BOTVINNIK: Without nuclear weapons, we will be nothing more than a rich, powerful Canada and an enormous Poland. *(A beat.)* There is a more important reason, as well.

HONEYMAN: Which is?

BOTVINNIK: The most exciting thing in the world is to know we can destroy the world. Like that. In a day. To know the bombs and the soldiers are in place. Their hands at the controls. The computers constantly running, monitoring, ready. We have never known such excitement. Alexander, Napoleon, Hitler would give up all of their conquests just to live in a world where such destruction is possible. Man has worked a long time for this. He is an animal who must fulfill every potential. Even the potential to kill himself. Even the potential to kill everything else.

HONEYMAN: It's simpleminded to say just because man *can* kill himself, that that's what he's going to do.

BOTVINNIK: It is? Look at the money, time and energy our governments put into making ready for war. What do we put into making ready for peace? You and me. That's all.

HONEYMAN: Governments have always armed themselves to the teeth, but mankind truly does hate war.

A WALK IN THE WOODS

BOTVINNIK: If mankind hated war, there would be millions of us and only two soldiers. *(A beat.)* Is this a serious enough conversation for you? Do you want to go on?

HONEYMAN: Not really.

BOTVINNIK: Perhaps we should go back then. *(Botvinnik starts out.)*

HONEYMAN: Wait.

BOTVINNIK: Yes.

HONEYMAN: What will you do about helping us?

BOTVINNIK: Nothing, of course.

HONEYMAN: Why not? I met your condition. I talked about trivial things...

BOTVINNIK: Brown suits? That was pitiful.

HONEYMAN: I'll try again.

BOTVINNIK: You're no good at it. You have no need for it.

HONEYMAN: I'll develop the need.

BOTVINNIK: Over time, yes. But now it only makes you uncomfortable.

HONEYMAN: Help us anyway.

BOTVINNIK: Why should I?

HONEYMAN: For the sake of peace.

BOTVINNIK: What kind of peace? Peace where you dominate? Peace where we dominate?

HONEYMAN: Peace where we share. You say man has to fulfill every potential—that he's that kind of animal. But he has other potentials—not just destructiveness. Andrey, man has the potential to become a whole new animal. One that trusts instead of fears. One that agrees when it makes sense to agree. That finds the way to live, because life has become for him—has *finally* become—a sacred thing.

BOTVINNIK: Only a child could believe this.

HONEYMAN: I believe it.

BOTVINNIK: Good. You will always be young. *(Botvinnik turns to go.)*

ZARA SPOOK AND OTHER LURES
by Joan Ackermann-Blount
A lake in New Mexico - Present - Talmadge (30's) - Mel (30's)

Talmadge - A man engaged to a champion bass fisherwoman
Mel - A slightly psychotic ex-husband of Ramona, another
    fisherwoman

Talmadge and Mel encounter one another on the banks of a lake
in New Mexico that is the sight of a bass fishing derby.
Talmade is going to marry Evelyn, a devoted fisherwoman
whom he suspects may be pregnant. As he speaks of Evelyn to
Mel, a man obsessed with finding his ex-wife, Ramona,
Talmadge reveals his great love for her. At first, Mel thinks
that Talmadge is talking about Ramona, not Evelyn, and
becomes jealous. The mistake is soon revealed, however, and
the two become friends.

(By the lake)
TALMADGE: *(Running up and down the shore, shouting, waving his
arms)* Evelyn! Evie! Get off the water! Lightning! It's gonna rain,
sweetheart, it's gonna pour! Evie, look up at the sky! Look up at the
sky! God forbid she should once in her life look up at the sky. There's
gonna be lightning! There is. It's storming up! Evie! Go back to the
marina! Oh God, please make her go back. Get rid of your pole!
Throw it out of the boat, it acts as a lightning rod, give it to Teale!
Why did I ever get her that pole in the first place, why didn't I just get
her that home entertainment center for her VCR I could have got it with
my green stamps go back to the marina! *(He runs and bumps into Mel;
screams)* I'm sorry. I didn't see you.
MEL: *(has rifle)* What's your trouble, boy?
TALMADGE: *(Trying to gain composure)* Nothing. Just someone out
there on the water.
MEL: There's someone out there on the water?
TALMADGE: Hm-mm.
MEL: Is that right?
TALMADGE: Uh-huh. They're fishing. She's fishing. There's a

tournament, a fishing tournament.

MEL: *(Nods)* Out on the water.

TALMADGE: Uh-huh.

MEL: How 'bout that.

TALMADGE: Actually, my wife is out in it, in the tournament, on the water, and I'm a little concerned.

MEL: You wife? That gal you're with is your wife?

TALMADGE: Well, no, not really, not yet, she's just my girlfriend now. Look, the little hairs on my arm are standing up.

MEL: They stand up every time you lie?

TALMADGE: They stand up when it's going to lightning. Have lightning. Be lightning.

MEL: That's why you're concerned about her. Your girlfriend.

TALMADGE: *(Tries to stay composed)* Yes, I am. I am. Concerned. *(Long pause)* Nice gun. *(Pause)* How 'bout those Oakland Raiders, huh? Is that Joe Montana something else? *(No response)* Well, I guess I better be going. Maybe I'll catch her in the next canyon.

MEL: What's your hurry, boy. Can't get out of life alive.

TALMADGE: See, she's pregnant. She doesn't believe it yet but she is. She is. Believe me.

MEL: You got her preganant?

TALMADGE: Yeah.

MEL: You got her pregnant?

TALMADGE: Yup, I did. All by my lonesome. *(in low tones)* Nice piece.

MEL: You lying again? *(Grabs him by the collar)*

TALMADGE: No. Why does everybody get so upset about it? It's a happy occasion. It's the life force.

MEL: You got my wife pregnant? *(Lifts up gun)*

TALMADGE: Your wife? Oh no, not your wife. I wouldn't dream of getting your wife pregnant. Look, could you please fire your gun a couple of times to try to get her attention over here. I haven't been able to get her attention. *(A loud thunder clap; Talmadge loses control and screams desperately:)* Evie! Evelyn!

MEL: *(Lets him go)* Evelyn? Who's Evelyn?

TALMADGE: Evelyn, get off the water!

MEL: Aren't you with Ramona?

TALMADGE: Please get off the water!

MEL: You picked Ramona up at the airport. I saw her get into your car with you.

TALMADGE: Evelyn! They're leaving, thank God. Goddammit it, that's not the way to the marina. That's the complete oppostite direction. Look, they're going the complete wrong direction. The other way! Evie, turn around! Turn around, honey! *(Another thunder clap)* Evie! *(Grabs Mel and starts crying shamelessly)* Oh, Jesus I don't want her to die. Evie...

MEL: *(Inadvertently comforting him)* She'll be all right.

TALMADGE: Every year someone dies on this lake from lightning.

MEL: No they don't.

TALMADGE: Yes they do.

MEL: Who told you that?

TALMADGE: *(Still crying)* Ramona. She's a friend of my wife's. I mean my girlfriend.

MEL: You can't believe her.

TALMADGE: *(Snivelling)* She's the world champion.

MEL: You can't believe her.

TALMADGE: Do you know her? You know Ramona? Does she lie?

MEL: Yeah, I know her. Look, pal, pull yourself together. Storms come through here all the time, no one gets hurt. Trust me, she'll be all right.

TALMADGE: I'll try. I'll try to trust you. Are you from this area? Do you know this area? You know people don't get hit by lightning every year?

MEL: Yeah.

TALMADGE: All right. Thank you so much. You're a sensitive man.

MEL: What did you call me?

TALMADGE: Uh...sorry, I didn't mean to offend you. Somone as tough as you...with a gun and all.

MEL: You said I was sensitive.

TALMADGE: I did. My apologies. You aren't sensitive.

MEL: I'm not?

TALMADGE: Are you?

MEL: You said I was.

TALMADGE: Is that all right?

MEL: Yeah. It's all right.

TALMADGE: Good.

MEL: I am a sensitive man.

TALMADGE: You know, you really are. You just might be the most sensitive man I've ever met.

MEL: Thank you. *(Looks at him, tears up, overwhelmed; pause)* You ever been to New Mexico before?

TALMADGE: No.

MEL: How do you like it?

TALMADGE: *(Smiles; still ingratiating)* I don't.

MEL: *(hasn't heard)* Uh-huh.

(Long awkward pause)

TALMADGE: You didn't happen to see that TV show last week where the woman was killed by a cement mixer? The other woman who saved her boy, knocked him out of the way, had a cerebral hemorhage, got her brain as a transplant? And then the husband came back?

MEL: No, I didn't catch that one.

TALMADGE: Mm. I missed the end. I was just wondering if the dead woman's personality came with her brain, or if the woman with the body was who that person was. *(Pause)* If the person was the brain or the body. If it was the brain I just wondered how the husband felt to come home and find someone else in his wife.

MEL: In his wife?

TALMADGE: But maybe it wasn't. Maybe it was just his wife who stayed in his wife; she just took over the new brain.

MEL: Hunh.

(Long pause)

MEL: You know, if I was to take a forked willow branch and hold it over that water right now it wouldn't budge.

TALMADGE: Really?

MEL: Only works on water underground.

TALMADGE: Huh.

MEL: Kind of like love. I tell people that, they don't understand.

TALMADGE: How's that?

MEL: When first you fall in love you get this wide open pretty view. Seems so easy. Before you know it that big open view shrinks up, you can't see a thing; all you can feel are those underground currents, driving you every which way, tearing up your insides.

TALMADGE: *(doesn't)* I see.

MEL: I knew you would.

(Long pause)

TALMADGE: Here, let me give you one of my cards. *(Reaches in wallet)* I'm Talmadge Slay. I'm with Byrobie, we're a young company but we're starting to make a mark with a new product called "Catch and Release" helps keep a fish alive through a stressful situation.

MEL: *(Hands him the beanie shooter, in exchange for the card)* Mel Graves. *(They shake hands.)*

TALMADGE: *(Nods)* Thank you.

(Pause; they both stare out at lake)

MEL: Well, you take care now, Talmadge.

TALMADGE: You too, Mel.

MEL: Sorry 'bout your face. *(Mel exits)*

TALMADGE: *(doesn't understand)* That's all right.

ZOYA'S APARTMENT
by Mikhail Bulgakov
translated by Nicholas Saunders and Frank Dwyer
Moscow - 1920's - Ametistov (28) - Abolyaninov (35)

Ametistov - A rascal
Abolyaninov - A fallen aristocrat

Ametistov is the rascally cousin of Zoya, a woman desperate to keep her Moscow apartment. Here, Ametistov teases Abolyaninov, a fallen aristocrat who must now grub for a living in post-revolutionary Moscow.

AMETISTOV: *(on the telephone)* Felicitations, Boris Semyonovich. How are you?... Oh, we're all busy, busy, busy!... So when can we...hic!...*pardon*, someone must be thinking of me...expect you?... No, no, no, secret, secret, secret! We have a surprise for you, Boris Semyonovich... My warmest regards! Goodbye. *(He hangs up.)* Hic!
ABOLYANINOV: He's an exceedingly vulgar man, don't you agree?
AMTISTOV: No, I don't. How can a man who earns five thousand rubles a month be considered vulgar? Hic!... Who is it? Who the hell wants me?... No, I respect Goose. After all, who has to drag himself around Moscow all day? You do.
AVOLYANINOV: Pardon me, Monsieur Ametistov, I do not "drag myself." I walk.
AMETISTOV: Here we go again. Don't be so sensitive! All right, all right, you walk, but Goose rides around in a fancy car. You sit in one room—*pardon, pardon*—perhaps the word "sit" is no longer used in high society—let's say you are "enthroned" in one little room. Goose has seven. You pound the piano—*pardon*, perform at the keyboard, I suppose—for a measly one hundred rubles a month. Goose takes home five thousand. You have to play, and Goose get to dance.
ABOLYANINOV: That's because this regime has made it impossible for decent people to survive.
AMESTISTOV: *Pardon, pardon!* Decent people can survive anything. I am a decent person, and I'm surviving. I arrived in Moscow without any pants, papa, and now...

206

ZOYA'S APARTMENT

ABOLYANINOV: Pardon me, what kind of "papa" am I to you, exactly?

AMETISTOV: Oh, don't be such a prig! "Papa." It's such a small thing...among men of our class...hic!

ABOLYANINOV: Excuse me, are you a really an aristocrat?

AMETISTOV: What a question! Can't you see for yourslf?...hic!... Damn it!

ABOLYANINOV: But I've never heard of the Ametistovs.

AMETISTOV: Oh, well, I'm sure there are plenty of perfectly good aristocratic names you've never heard of! It's known to every single perosn in the Penza province! Oh, *signor*! If you only know what I had to endure at the hands of the Bolsheviks, your hair would stand on end...First they looted our estate, then they put my chateau to the torch...

ABOLYANINOV: And where, exactly, was this chateau?

ABOLYANINOV: My chateau? You're asking about my chateau?

ABOLYANINOV: Yes. The one they put to the torch...

AMETISTOV: Oh, that chateau...in, uh...oh, I don't even want to think about it—it's still too painful! White columns...yes, it's all coming back to me. *Un, deux, trois...vier, funf, sechs*...seven. Seven columns, each more beautiful than the last. Oh, why go on aobut it? And my wonderful cattle! With their pedigrees! And my brickworks!

ABOLYANINOV: My aunt Varvara Nikolaevna had such fine stallions...

AMETISTOV: Your Aunt Varvara! I had one myself, and it was terrific! What's the matter with you, anyway? Cheer up, papa.

ABOLYANINOV: I'm so sad today...

AMETISTOV: Me, too! Can you believe it? I wonder why? Maybe it's some kind of premonition... The best cure for sadness is a game of cards!

ABOLYANINOV: I don't care for cards. I like horses. I had a horse called Pharoah... *(We hear a voice raised in song: "They remind me...")* ...a red jacket with yellow sleeves, and a black bandolier— Pharoah...

AMETISTOV: I love faro, what a game!... The dealer turns up the

207

corner of the card, and you, papa, break out in a cold sweat. And then, at the most exciting moment, whap!—you've got yourself a winner and his little card lies there on the table as it it has been cut down by a scythe!... Maybe it's Aliluya who has upset me so... My God, if only I could get away from here!

ABOLYANINOV: Yes, as soon as possible. I can't go on living here.

AMETISTOV: Hold on, little brother. In three months we'll be on our way to Nice! Have you ever been to Nice, Count!

ABOLYANOV: Yes, many times.

AMETISTOV: ...Me, too. In early childhood. Oh, the memories! My late mother used to take me there. From our chateau. Two governesses went with us. Not counting the nanny. What curly hair I had in those days! I wonder...are there any cardsharps in Monte Carlo?

ABOLYANINOV: I don't know... *(sadly)* ...I don't know anything any more...

AMETISTOV: You really are sad, aren't you, Count? What a funny man you are. Well, my companion, before Zoyechka gets here, shall we sneak away to the "Bavaria"?

ABOLYANINOV: But that's just a common beerhall, filthy, disgusting...

AMETISTOV: You obviously haven't seen the lobsters they got in yesterday! Each lobster was the size of...I don't want to exaggerate...the size of a guitar! Shall we go, papachka?

ABOLYANINOV: All right, let's go.

210